POLITICAL EDUCATION —
A Practical Guide for Christian Youth Workers

*Produced in conjunction with the
Frontier Youth Trust*

POLITICAL EDUCATION

A Practical Guide for Christian Youth Workers

by

Fred Milson Ph.D.

Exeter
The Paternoster Press

ISBN:
Casebound: 0 85364 257 5
Study Edition: 0 85364 258 3

AUSTRALIA:
*Emu Book Agencies Pty., Ltd.,
63, Berry St., Granville, 2142, N.S.W.*

SOUTH AFRICA:
*Oxford University Press,
P.O. Box 1141, Cape Town*

British Library Cataloguing in Publication Data

Milson, Fred
  Political education.
  1. Christian education
  2. Politics — Study and teaching
  3. Christianity and politics
  I. Title
  320'.07   BV1485

  ISBN 0-85364-257-5
  ISBN 0-85364-258-3 Pbk

Produced in conjunction with Frontier Youth Trust

*Typeset by Photoprint, Paignton, Devon
and Printed in Great Britain for the Paternoster Press,
Paternoster House, 3 Mount Radford Crescent, Exeter, Devon
by Butler & Tanner Ltd., Frome, Somerset.*

To my Number Two grandson, Michael Blaszkowicz,
with the hope that when he grows up, he will
be interested in both Christianity and politics.

CONTENTS

Preface

Two years ago the Joseph Rowntree Charitable Trust gave me a grant for research into political education in voluntary youth movements. As the churches and the inter-denominational organizations are still major partners in Youth Service, much of my evidence has come from these sources. My enquiries through letters, literature and visits have made one or two things clear. The first is that there is a widespread interest in the subject linked with a conviction that Christian education ought to include attempts to help young people to understand the political realities of their time and to equip them to take a more active part in political activity if they wish.

The second feature is a confusion about the issues involved. Part of this is due to the fact that we are all using the same words with different meanings. But equally significant is the communication gap between those who write about the subject — both theologians and political scientists — and those who want to relate these ideas to education programmes in a local unit. Typical is the experience of a Girls' Brigade captain concerned to promote a programme of political education for the girls in her company. She wrote to the acknowledged sources. 'They sent me a book list suitable for university graduates.' She then wrote to her M.P. who sent her a C.O.I. book on the British Parliament — 'very good but too deep!' Finally, I have discovered many leaders who have the will but lack the skill, who want to help their members to understand their world better but confess that they lack the 'know-how'.

This book is written with these three findings in mind. It seeks to respond to the widespread interest in the subject, to clarify and simplify the main issues and to offer practical suggestions for programmes. This book aims to be a primer on political education for Christian youth groups, and should be judged as such — I am not competent to write anything more technical or sophisticated. Running through it is a theme, a signature tune, which is played so often that it may appear monotonously repetitious. It is that in this matter of the political education of young Christians, the local church and the local unit are the key to progress since they represent the greatest need and the greatest opportunity. My excuse is that I have to keep playing this record if I am to be loyal to the findings of my research.

Fred Milson

1
The Church and Politics

A recurring question

A few years ago, in East Berlin, and on successive days, I met and talked with two Protestant pastors. I was curious to know how Christians live in a state that is avowedly atheistic and to say the least, discourages the practice of religion and the propagation of the gospel. These two men, living in the same situation, adopted very different attitudes to the "powers that be". The first adhered to the Lutheran doctrine that the church and the state are separate, each with its own function, respectively spiritual and political, and neither should seek to interfere with the other. It is a view which finds support in Paul. "Remind them to be submissive to the government and the authorities, to obey them" (Titus 3:1, NEB): and in Peter, "Submit yourself to every human institution for the sake of the Lord" (1 Peter 2:13, NEB). So I asked him, "If I were preaching in your church next Sunday and said, 'If Marx is right then Christ is wrong: if Christ is right than Marx is wrong', what would happen to me?" He paused for thought and then replied, "It is a hypothetical question since you do not have a licence from the authorities to preach in East Berlin."

By contrast, the second man said he was sorry for me, living in a country where the government did not disapprove of my Christian profession, since this could so easily lead to a formal adherence rather than a constant challenge. According to him, the Christian in an atheistic country should engage in a continual dialogue with the authorities, sometimes approving the actions of a monolithic state and sometimes daring to criticize. He was living dangerously; he challenged the "powers that be";

he displayed a daily heroism. And he too, of course, can find scriptural support for his stance: "Peter replied for himself and the Apostle, 'We must obey God rather than men' " (Acts 5:9, NEB).

These examples are not quoted to pronounce judgement. Both were sincere men acting according to their conscience which, in each case, had been brought under the scrutiny of Christ: in this sense, both were right. In East Germany, strong pressures are brought by the state to persuade every young person to join the "Free German Youth Movement", the official state-run youth organization, whose sessions include teaching which is Marxist and unsympathetic to a Christian view of life. Wisely, both the Catholic and Protestant churches in East Germany have said that they leave it to the individual conscience of young Christians whether or not they join the "Free German Youth Movement", and have announced that they will give support to those making either decision, whether they face indoctrination or possible loss of opportunities for higher education and diminished career prospects.

The two German Protestant pastors have been introduced here for another reason. They illustrate in an unfamiliar situation not only the complexity of political decisions Christians have to make, but that there is no blue-print to guide us. It belongs to the freedom with which we have been endowed by God, that political choice is not for us an "open-and-shut" case. Contrary commitments can find equal justification in the Scriptures and indeed depend on many other factors, temperament and circumstances among them.

The Church is constantly exhorted today to become more involved with political issues. We are asked how we can go on being pre-occupied with personal evangelism, ritual and organization, when there are urgent matters like racism, poverty, bureaucracy and conservation to attend to. But these well-intentioned advisers miss the point. Inevitably, and from the beginning, the Church has been involved with politics. The first Roman citizen to be converted to Christianity had to face the dilemma of loyalty to Christ and loyalty to Caesar. With the original piece of property that the Church owned, it entered as an organization into the political arena. But everybody knows that the link between church and state became close and sophisticated. For many centuries, the political history of

Europe is quite inseparable from its church history. After Constantine, power was shared between Emperor and Pope, with a recurring see-saw of the balance. A sixth century mosaic in Ravenna depicts the Emperor Justinian, with a halo, and his bishop as one of the servants of the court, standing obediently beside his master. On other occasions, the Pope proved to be more powerful than the Emperor, particularly after the discovery, by Ambrose of Milan, that the threat of excommunication was a powerful sanction ensuring the obedience even of earthly rulers. Hildebrand, Pope Gregory VII (1020-1085), compelled Emperor Henry IV to sue for pardon in the famous scene at Canossa at the end of January 1077.

The reason for this brief excursion is to make a single point. Ask not for the Church to become involved with politics. It is and always has been. Ask rather what is to be the nature of that involvement given the eternal gospel and the contemporary facts.

There are several possible broad perspectives open to us. But first I shall describe one which though sometimes tried in the past, is not an option for us today. It is that Christians should rule the State, should exercise the political power. This attempt has taken one of two forms. Either there has been a theocracy, in which God is seen as the direct ruler of the State; there is no distinction between sin and crime; the laws of the land are the laws of God. John Calvin attempted this in Geneva and so did the Pilgrim Fathers in Massachusetts. The other form finds a good exemplar in Charlemagne (742-814). Here a powerful monarch, of Christian persuasion, considered that he reigned by divine will, gave the church a large part to play in the life of the state, encouraged Christian institutions and passed what were believed to be Christian laws.

That this course is no longer possible or even desirable, is plain and undeniable. We live in a pluralist society where there is no longer one single faith or point of view which alone is socially acceptable. Most Christians see this clearly enough, but we do not always see the consequences which follow. We can no longer press for legislation which assumes that everybody in Britain is Christian or even accepts the Christian ethical code. We may be leaven, but our faith alone does not give us the right to be leaders. We are not the "establishment" any longer. Christ does not come to us today packaged and gift-wrapped by our culture. We may witness, but we may not legislate. In an increasingly secularized society, we have to learn how to operate as a minority movement, with fewer and fewer special advantages, allowing Christian voices to be heard along with the others. (This is part of what we mean by the word "secularization".) There are many signs that the churches find it difficult to adjust to this new role.

There are however more feasible approaches. They differ widely, but each could find support in two areas. They have all been tried somewhere at some time in the long history of the Church. And, if we search long enough in the Scriptures, we can find one text at least — perhaps torn from its context — which can plausibly be used in justification.

(i) Some Christians argue for non-involvement. On this view, the world is incorrigibly an evil place. You must use it, but have as little to do with it as possible lest you be corrupted by it — a caution particularly necessary with politics. This view is associated sometimes with monasticism, and commonly with pietism, individualism, other-worldliness, and escapism. It applies the "closed-shop" principle to those who are regarded as the children of God, though within the narrow confines of the movement it can develop immense moral strength. Today many traditional Christians favour a massive concentration on evangelism and personal salvation. The attitude of non-involvement, of despair about the world of affairs, may be associated with a variety of theological and ethical attitudes. One is eschatological — the belief that the end of the world is near, the old order passes away, so why bother? Another is a "Moral Rearmament" approach that nothing is worth devoting your energy to except the moral and spiritual reform of the individual — working for a new social and political order is like shuffling a greasy pack of playing cards. Another attitude probably owes much to Eastern mysticism: this present life and the world are supremely unimportant, nothing here matters and salvation lies in escaping from it and in the death of interest and desire. All those attitudes can be found among Christians and often among the members of the same congregation. They are (to repeat a point) supported by an eclectic choice of biblical texts. "And therefore 'Come away and leave them, separate yourselves' says the Lord" (2 Cor. 6:17, NEB). On this model the church is a gathered community which has been rescued from an evil world.

"Their unbelieving minds are so blinded by the god of this passing age, that the gospel of the glory of God . . . cannot dawn
upon them and bring them light" (2 Cor. 4:4, NEB).

So behind the refusal of Christians to become involved with
the politics of the day as part of their Christian discipleship, lie
images of the world as hostile, evil, irrelevant and tempting, or
as a diversion from the real tasks of believers. Machiavelli
(1467-1527) represents a variation. The world and its political
systems are ruled by their own godless laws. Christians should
learn what these are and use them to gain power.

(ii) By complete contrast, there have always been Christians
prepared to accept the political structures as essentially
God-given, though not without some need of reform. Paul, for
example, had a great respect for the civil order that was
provided by Roman rule and in several places suggests that it is
part of divine providence. Those who have followed this aspect
of Pauline emphasis have always contributed largely to the
stability of their societies. At their worst, they suspect that any
suggestion of revolution must emanate from an atheistic source.
As Max Weber pointed out,[1] Protestant Christians often
prosper through their sober lives and habits of thrift and in-
dustriousness, and so they often come to have a stake in the
economic and political establishment. Perhaps the most
notorious instance of this approach was the period in American
history when, according to Galbraith,[2] capitalism was equated
with the will of God. But at its best, the attitude contributes to
law and order without which civilized life is impossible. Its
weakness is that it will often tolerate injustice for the sake of
stability, to stop the boat from rocking; it makes a wilderness
and calls it peace; it is a form of negative involvement in the
politics of the day since it tends to favour support of the powers
that be. And the claim can be made that this is an aspect of
discipleship since one would expect to find Christians among the
more reliable and respectable members of any community.

(iii) Finally, some Christians think their faith involves them
in a struggle to transform their society in the direction of
freedom and justice. Unlike the first group they do not wholly
despair of the world. On the contrary, they see it as the arena of
God's activity where he grapples with evil, in individual lives
and social and political structures alike; and where he seeks the
co-operation of Christ's followers. But unlike the second group,

they are not happy with the world as it is and concentrate their attention on those aspects of society which are clearly a rejection of God's rule. There are many powerful and persuasive advocates of this view today. They are happy to be called "Christian revolutionaries", and promise a new life-style for the Church. They rally us to fight against the evil in the structure of society, against the malevolent non-personal forces. "Right politics is religion."[3] "Every Catholic who is not a revolutionary and who is not on the side of revolutionaries is in mortal sin" (Father Camilo Torres, a Bolivian priest, subsequently killed in a clash with the security forces). For them, a large part of our Christian duty is to make life better for the poor and oppressed and this means political activity.

My heart and mind incline to this latter view. (So, despite my earlier non-judgemental statement, I support the second Berlin pastor). And it seems to me to reflect the underlying biblical message as distinct from isolated proof texts. But I have considerable misgivings about some of the things that I hear the Christian revolutionaries say. For political activity is by no means the whole of our Christian duty. Nor should we invest too heavily in it. And we have to guard against unrealistic hopes in this fallen world, against fantasy, against utopianism, as well as against despair. Nor should we suppose that our efforts in this direction will lead to many people becoming Christians. Men cannot be saved by social engineering, thank God, and a favourable social environment will not guarantee their mental and moral health. We have already seen that when the oppressed are emancipated they too easily become the oppressors. Parks, the sociologist, had a salutary story of a slave who was freed and the first thing he did with his freedom was to buy himself a slave. As Christians we should fight the evil structures, but without illusions. We fight for justice, not for individual righteousness. Slums obscure the face of God, but suburbia does not inevitably reveal him.

Among Christians who wish to be involved in politics, there is a group of people who are — if it is not horribly patronising to say so — noble but naive. They operate on the principle of "All you need is love". They consider that there can be some direct application of Christian love to complicated social and political issues; that somehow Christians have an instant solution; that they are absolved from the necessity to do their political

homework. Consider the recent history — moving but sad — of
the Peace Movement, in Ulster. So long as it was an emotional
appeal, the movement flourished. But as soon as it moved
necessarily into the area of hard political choices, support fell
away. We live in a world where individual goodness will not inevitably lead to new political systems. Christians have no
panacea. Sadly we have to admit that much harm in this world
has resulted from the efforts of those who have zeal without
knowledge. Indeed, the attempts to apply over-simplified moral
solutions to political problems can be counter-productive, as
President Carter has discovered since he took office. On the
social front we fight, not for love, but for rough justice at best,
though we may still see Christ casting out the demons from
individual lives.

With these misgivings, I am on the side of the Christian
revolutionaries. It is from this perspective that the book has
been written.

An original dilemma
"It wor all green fields when I wor a lad", sings Stanley
Holloway. Nostalgia creeps upon most of us at some time and
we escape from present dilemmas by looking at the past through
rosy-coloured spectacles. Christians are not immune from this
temptation. And our nostalgia takes a particular form. Faced
with the hard political choices described in the last section, we
want to go back in imagination to the first days of Christianity.
The waters are muddy now, but higher up the mountain, near
the source, the river is crystal-clear and uncorrupted. Christianity began with Christ and the disciples and we think all will be
made plain if we return to the origins. Somewhere along the
line, the faith was disastrously changed by Paul or Constantine
or the Roman Catholic Church. Nearly all the reforming
movements in the history of the church have not been primarily
concerned dynamically to meet a new situation. They were
directed — as in the case of Luther and Wesley among others —
to recover the original impetus and style: to return to "the pit
from which we were dug."

However, when we read the original documents, we find the
dilemma is present from the beginning. (This will be a shock only to those Christians who suppose that God wants us to have a
quiet life, and never argue among ourselves or with the world.

But Christ stated explicitly tht he came not to bring peace but a sword). We are not in fact given a blue-print for our involvement with the world. From the beginning Christians had the awesome freedom and responsibility to work it out for themselves on the basis of the fact of Christ. When he was asked a specific question on the subject — "Are we or are we not permitted to pay taxes to the Roman Emperor?" — he replied, "Pay Caesar what is due to Caesar and pay God what is due to God." (Luke 20: 21-26, NEB). It was a characteristically quick and ready answer. Did he smile when he gave it because he saw through the trap?

But it is no blue-print about Christian involvement with the political powers since it makes no pronouncement on the question that believers have pondered over and argued about ever since the original statement was made. "What is it that belongs to Caesar and what is it that belongs to God? We have a duty to both, it is clear, but where do we draw the line?" Once again Christ has answered the question but not in a way that settles the issue; he prompts us to further questioning, to deeper exploration on our own behalf.

Dietrich Bonhoeffer[4] (1906-1945) has made a profound impression on the post-war world. He was at once learned theologian, devout disciple and political activist. And all this was rooted in a way of seeing and experiencing life which was for him spontaneous and natural. From all the accounts of his friends, he was a delightful companion, thoroughly at home in this world, enjoying its good gifts. By sheer friendliness, he won over some of his prison warders. He was in complete sympathy with the world of beauty and tradition and yet at the same time, touched by the Eternal. But when the moment came, he did not hold back from joining a plot to assassinate Hitler, and all as part of his Christian duty. And in the end — when his aged parents and fiancée were threatened with arrest — he explained that he was an enemy of National Socialism and his objections were rooted in the Christian faith. Inspired by Christ, he moved into the field of political involvement, but without any divine mandate for a particular course of action, which he had to work out for himself. The view that the Gospel gives us precise instructions about what to do under any circumstances he described as the doctrine of rusty swords.

This section has been written to comment on a perplexity

which often arises for us Christians. There are few among us now who would say that our faith has nothing to do with politics. A larger group would think that the Church should struggle only against any state that will not permit worship. But the fastest growing group is those Christians who think that we have some sort of gospel for the society in which we live, however secularized it may have become. At this point many of us encounter frustration, disappointment and perplexity. For it is by no means clear which path we should tread and there is no light from heaven. We have the will to be involved but lack the precise guidance. Then to add to the confusion we notice that Christians of equal wisdom and piety make conflicting choices. In few countries of the world is there an obvious political alignment, a course of action for all Christians. Some Christians make political choices which give economic justice the priority; others choose personal freedom as the main concern. Some are pacifists, others support increased expenditure on defence. And so on. No doubt as with others, temperamental factors affect believers' choices; and no doubt also, *pace* Karl Marx, our own interests affect unconsciously the choices we make. But many of us would claim that we are also guided in those choices by Christian perspectives.

Sometimes, in this welter of differences and dilemmas, we are tempted to feel that if only we could get back to the first days of the faith all would be plain: that there would be one obvious policy for us, if only we were Christian enough; surely then there would be one Christian party to join. Not so. If the first disciples had joined political parties, they would not all have belonged to the same one. The dilemma has been there from the beginning. That we have to make our own choice in the light of Christian principles and the "life-situation" — this is evidence of the freedom and humanity with which God has endowed us; that Christians are driven by their faith to join different parties or support different parties only illustrates the versatility of God.

This matter is only one aspect of a paradox that lies at the heart of the Christian faith which is at once world-affirming and world-denying, this-worldly and other-worldly, disciplined and fulfilling. "I am come that men may have life and may have it in all its fulness" (John 10:10, NEB), says Christ. But he also says, "If anyone wishes to be a follower of mine he must leave self behind'' (Matthew 16:24, NEB). The rewards and duties begin now but they stretch into eternity. Our responsibilities are exhausted neither by working hard to make this earth a better place to live in nor by ensuring that a few more shall enjoy the splendours of eternal bliss. We have to fight on both fronts. Christians are called to be in the world but not of the world. ''I pray thee not to take them out of the world but to keep them from the evil one'' (John 17:15, NEB). The same situation was described at greater length but no less felicitously, in the *Epistle to Diognetus.*

> Christians are not distinguished from the rest of mankind either in locality or in speech or in customs. For they dwell not somewhere in cities of their own, neither do they use some different language, nor practise an extraordinary kind of life . . . But while they dwell in the cities of Greeks and barbarians as the lot of each is cast, and follow the native customs in dress and food and the other arrangements of life, yet the constitution of their own citizenship, which is set forth, is marvellous, and confessedly contradicts expectations. They dwell in their own countries, but only as sojourners; they bear their share in all things as citizens, and they endure all hardships as strangers. Every foreign country is a fatherland to them and every fatherland is foreign . . . They obey the established laws, and they surpass the laws in their own lives.

The passage describes a creative and perplexing relationship between the Christian and the secular powers. And when, confronted by modern challenges, it is enlarged to include political activity for desirable change, we have a picture of hopeful Christian involvement in the worldly affairs of men. Those who think there is something more than this world often begin to find the world even more precious. But further, by a strange paradox, it is often those who consider that we have here no abiding city who work hardest to improve the sewage system and the water supply of the city where they live.

Impressive are the lives of those active in the affairs of men because they believe this world is important but not all: whose conviction is a significant shift from T. E. Lawrence's ''Nothing matters''. They believe everything matters but nothing matters absolutely.

Christianity does not offer us a distinctive political programme and repeated attempts of politicians to claim God's support for their programmes are always embarrassing.

(Though from time to time there arise specific issues, like racism, on which one may expect a consensus of Christian politics.) But in modern societies there can be no such thing as a "Christian political party" and attempts to create such in Europe and elsewhere have not been encouraging. Nor is there any such animal as a "Christian politician" just as there cannot be a "Christian engineer". There can of course be a politician (and an engineer) who is also a Christian; and his faith will have a profound effect upon his hopes and endeavours in his professional work. Christians are called, in my view, to be political activists, but they are not given a detailed manifesto. They have two main sources of raw material. One is the fact of Christ, his teaching, example and saving grace. The other is their social and political environment. God has trusted the faithful to work out for themselves how they should relate to the world. And so it has been from the beginning.

Has the Church always favoured reaction?
In revolutionary circles, the incursion of Christians into politics will be regarded with a mixture of cynicism, suspicion and amusement. The reaction will almost certainly owe something, at least indirectly, to the Marxist view of religion. "Religion is the sigh of the oppressed creature, the heart of a heartless world, just as it is the heart of an unspiritual world. It is the opium of the people" (Karl Marx).

According to this view, religion encourages the working-classes to be content with their lot: the rituals of religion divert people from their proper revolutionary tasks. Here, the religious attitude to life, by its nature, is seen as dedicated to stability rather than revolution: it works with a model of social integration, not a model of change; it is consensus rather than conflict: law and order is preferred to justice and freedom. Marxists do not expect to find Christians on the frontiers of a dynamic society, and do not look for them on the barricades. As the Duke of Wellington observed — in any strategy one should not underestimate the enemy. There is undeniable substance in these strictures. Christians are expected to bring forth treasures new and old but they seem to be programmed for the latter. Once Christians obtain any power in a secular society, their religion is infected with a fatal tendency to defend the status quo including their own privileges and possessions.

There are many examples in the past and the present. In some cases, the attempts to make religious organizations and activities a bulwark of stability and tradition are overt and acknowledged. When Hannah More (1745-1833) began schools for poor children, she was quite explicit about her intentions. She operated at a time when the civilized world had been shaken by Thomas Paine's *Rights of Man*. She sought to persuade the poor, in the language of ingenuous homeliness, to embrace habits of humanity, soberness, industry, thrift and respect for God and all forms of established authority (cf *Village Politics,* 1792). Her education programmes were partly designed to reconcile the poor to their lot: civilization, she judged, depended upon the existence of a large and permanent body of poor people. Hannah More was a Christian intervening on the political scene at the behest of her faith, but largely in terms of law and order. So she describes how she tried to persuade her neighbours in a Cheddar parish to support her schemes:

> "I said I had a little plan which I hoped would secure their orchards from being robbed, their rabbits from being shot, their poultry from being stolen, and which might lower the poor-rates."[5]

Elsewhere the over-commitment of Christians to stability, tradition, law and order in the social and political structure has been covert, and far less self-conscious and deliberate. The Church of England used to be described as "the Conservative Party at prayer", though there is far less force in the gibe now. But the identification was not usually part of a planned policy: given the prevailing values and the circumstances, it was inevitable and predictable. Likewise, the political parties on the Continent who have incorporated "Christian" in their title — like the Christian Democrats in West Germany — have become the national equivalent of the Tory Party in Britain. But they did not begin by Christians saying they ought to belong to the party of stability rather than reform. Although church people in this country are more inclined to vote Tory than Labour, it is hard to measure how much this owes to religious conservatism, since religious affiliation is linked with two other factors also associated with the likelihood of Tory voting — being old and living in the country.

Whilst we are in the confessional box let us admit something else. Not only have Christians tended to favour stability, to the relative neglect of necessary change, but even those Christians renowned for their efforts to secure certain reforms have often been reactionary in their attitudes to other contemporary evils. So John Wesley (1703-1791) worked for the abolition of slavery but opposed the efforts of the American colonists to secure release from tyranny in the War of Independence. William Wilberforce (1759-1833) also fought against slavery but shortly before his death he said that the first Reform Act was too radical. Like other famous Christians who intervened in public affairs, they were not consistent radicals: they tended to concentrate on one or two reforms rather than interpreting the gospel as a challenge to the existing system.

All this is true. The majority of Christians and their leaders have belonged to the conformists in the community certainly since the first days when it became socially acceptable to be a follower of Christ. And still today our critics are right to ask whether Christians are not inclined to become terribly worried about individual sins whilst ignoring the far more serious crimes committed by whole societies. In a famous piece of sociological analysis, R. K. Merton[6] has given a list of individual responses to the American ''anomie''. How do people behave when there is a socially acceptable goal for everybody — i.e. to be a success and make a lot of money — but there is not open for everybody — e.g. the blacks, the very poor, the less gifted — a socially acceptable means to achieve the goal?

(i) The conformists go along with the situation and they are almost always in the majority. They accept goals and means.
(ii) The innovators gain the cultural goals but by means which, if they were publicly exposed, would not be approved. They indulge in sharp practice, if not criminal activity. They approve the goal but not the means.
(iii) The ritualists. They don't like the goal and often criticize it but they have to play along. They reject the goal in a sense but use the means. ''Don't aim high and you won't be disappointed.'' ''I'm satisfied with what I've got.''
(iv) The retreatists. These are the various kinds of drop-outs — nihilists, anarchists, drug-addicts — who reject society as it is and therefore both its goals and aims. ''Stop the world — I want to get off.''
(v) The rebels. Merton here describes the constructive revolu-

tionaries who discriminate between the goals and the means they accept or reject. They want to change the world but not by first destroying it. They approve of some things but want to change others by constitutional means.

Christians have been and are represented in all five of these categories of social attitudes. For example, the anchorites, who withdrew from the world, were an example of the fourth group. But through the ages and today, the majority of Christians are conformists, and so whilst ensuring stability, they may perpetuate the evils of society. (There are encouraging signs that an increasing number of Christians, especially among the young, are rebels in the Merton definition).

All this is true and more. But it leaves something to be said on the other side. For one thing, even those Christian leaders — like Wesley and William Booth — who concentrate on the conversion of the individual will indirectly have a profound effect on the social scene. To change people is one step towards changing society. Moreover — and this was particularly true in the case of William Booth — the effort to save souls rapidly brings the evangelist up against the necessity to make better provision for their bodies.

But in my view, there is a yet more important point. God never leaves himself without prophetic witness. However dark it seems, the voice of Christ speaks through the prophets in judgement and mercy on the contemporary scene. And let us make no mistake — at certain periods in church history and Christian civilization, terrible cruelties have been and are wrought upon people, often in the name of Christ. In Czarist Russia, the priests frequently collaborated with the authorities to impose severe penalties for trivial offences; Victorian factory and mine owners went regularly to church. Ignorance and poverty have sometimes been encouraged by the church in order to keep the people in subservience. But always there have been the prophets and the future belonged to them: from out of utter darkness comes the light. Ambrose of Milan (340-392) challenged the ruthless cruelty of an Emperor and brought him to public penitence. Wycliffe (1328-84) dared to challenge the authority of the Church in temporal affairs. When the Conquistadors were enslaving the inhabitants of South America in the name of the gospel, there were not lacking a few priests to protest in the name of that same gospel. Savonarola (1452-98) was excommunicated and executed for denouncing the immorality of the papal court. That is how God works. He speaks through chosen individuals rather than through institutions or directly to the masses. Evil is given a long rope but is never entirely untroubled by the prophetic voices who call for change. There is enough evidence to persuade me at least, that reactionary attitudes do not belong to the essence of the gospel.

Recently, as a visiting lecturer in Belfast, I was asked the question, "How radical may the Christian be?" For once I think it would have been fair to reply that the question is wrong. For there can be no limits to Christian radicalism: the level should be decided by the radicalism demanded by the situation we confront, not by a personal commitment to radicalism or conservatism. In present world circumstances the right question to ask is, "How much force — physical and non-physical — are you prepared to use to effect necessary change?" As other reformers, Christians must attend to the mechanics of revolution as well as its ideas. On the extreme Left — of which the international terrorists are the most outrageous advocates — are those who say that the present system cannot be changed without bombs and shootings. Anything else, they judge, is sentimental liberalism. So they have no qualms of conscience about shooting a pilot or hijacking a plane which includes innocent children among the passengers. These acts of violence, they say, are chicken-feed compared with the bigger atrocities of imperialism and capitalism. The end justifies the means. What is the life of one child compared with the thousands who are suffering in Palestinian refugee camps? To these fanatics, Christians must find answers that are more than handwringing exercises. "How much violence will you accept?" is the key question.

In some countries under Fascist domination, it is hard to see how change can be effected without resort to arms. Secure in democratic Europe, do we have any right to criticize those priests in South American countries who join in armed struggle for a bit more justice and freedom? Christians may share the bitterness even of the terrorists. Something has gone tragically wrong with this world. We too feel alienated from aspects of our society. Many countries display vicious features of exploitation and tyranny. Christians may share too the strong desire to see change and improvement. Their quarrel with the extremists is mainly about the means. How much force is permitted? And of what kind? Christians wonder how effective violence is. There is a case for saying that bloody revolution creates at least as many evils as it cures. Karl Popper has asked this question: Is it not better in the long run for human welfare and happiness to take problems one by one, rather than work to a grand strategy? Are some of the extremists, notably the terrorists, projecting their personal problems on the world situation? We all display a tendency to follow this practice. One enquiry arises distinctively from a Christian perspective. Should anybody be as convinced as the terrorists that they and they alone are right? Is not that trying to play God? Is it not a form of idolatry? Paradoxically, Christians can agree with those who say that the world is saved by its lack of faith. The worst crimes in history have been commited, by those people, like Hitler, who had no doubts.

All this we may say and more. But none of it gives room for complacency. For the outpourings of the terrorists, irrational though they be, leave us with two uncomfortable issues. First, if we rely for change upon persuasion, the secret ballot-box, and always keep strictly to constitutional practice, how effective shall we be? Can any revolution, any alternative society, be attained by a major reliance on pamphlets and discussion? And even if we are successful in contributing to a change in public attitudes, will not the process be so slow as to be ineffective? Minority groups are listened to and gain concessions when they acquire arms. Is "Christian humanism and liberalism" a river of perfectionism that runs out in the sands of futility? If we do succeed, will it be before a whole deprived generation has passed away? And will not the villainous supporters of the present system (whoever they are) laugh at our naivety and even perhaps send funds for our work? The second issue is even more serious. Nobody in a modern state can eschew the use of force and violence (used here in the sense of physical force), because he is constantly being protected by it. The relative peace and security of pacifists in Northern Ireland is protected by the presence of the British armed forces. Law and order is provided for all of us by the police who use force and on some occasions are driven to use violence. Another kind of force is used by governments to protect society, as when the firemen go on strike for high wages and the troops are brought in. Propaganda is an insidious kind of force. Nobody can contract out of some dependence upon the use of force and it begins to look a little hypocritical when we talk as though we can.

This is far from meaning that we must agree with the extremists, still less with the terrorists. After their most vituperative passages on the use of violence in "Fascist imperialist régimes", we are still permitted to ask whether two wrongs will make a right. But it does mean that, "How radical may a Christian be?" (or for that matter "How conservative may a Christian be?"), is not the right question. We have to bring our reliance upon force, and even violence (physical damage to persons), under the scrutiny and the law of Christ. The real question for us is how we can humanize the use of force. Doing that will not be easy. And different Christians will give different answers. But at least it may demonstrate that radicals are not necessarily people who want to throw bombs, kidnap industrialists or hijack planes.

Equally we may persuade a few that the hour has come to question the unthinking acceptance (by the majority of churchgoers) of "law and order" as the supreme goals of Christian political involvement. It is high time that "justice and freedom" gained a hearing, not only in Geneva, but in every Bethel and parish church and Christian home throughout the land. It is worth considering whether the frequent and persistent over-identification of the Christian churches with the status quo has not rested on two errors. The first is to give a universal rather than a contemporary significance to Paul's argument in Romans 13 — "Let every soul be in subjection to the higher powers . . ." That made a lot of sense when Roman law and order often facilitated the spread of the gospel but does it have the same authority where Christians live under a Fascist régime today?[9] The second possible error is that the churches have often overlooked the profound significance of the identification of Jesus with the poor and powerless.[10]

Politics without political education
From one point of view, there cannot have been a time in its long history when the Church appeared to be more involved with politics than it is at present. There is no major public issue on which it has not made statements — abortion, poverty, racial

discrimination, homelessness, and so on. Christian leaders are required to read their newspapers as regularly and carefully as they read their Bibles. The officials of the World Council of Churches have their eyes on the ends of the earth. Nothing escapes their attention though they are suspected of being far more severe on the denial of human rights in countries like South Africa than in countries of the Communist bloc, like the U.S.S.R. Christians from the Third World have introduced European and American Christians to the theology of conflict, confrontation and crisis. Many of their pronouncements demonstrate a belief that God is at the centre of the struggle for justice, peace and freedom, wherever it is waged. Many church-goers however, think that the church as a global organization has become over-involved with politics and thereby secularized the gospel. It is the present contention however that it would be impossible for the church to become "over-involved" with the world since involvement is another word for the identification which lies at the heart of the gospel. But we ought to ask questions about the nature of our involvement.

A whole library of books has been written out of this interest. There are major works like Alan Richardson's *The Political Christ* and innumerable pamphlets of which the British Council of Churches series, *Britain Today and Tomorrow,* is the latest example. Excellent as all this is from our point of view, it suffers from one fatal defect; it offers a lot of politics with very little political education. Despite strenuous efforts to share the vision, it remains a hope that is discussed enthusiastically in the board room of the church without making much impression on the people who work on the shop floor, the vast army of non-professional Christians. All these pronouncements and books have not significantly changed the life-style of Christians in this country. For most of us, religion remains largely a matter of individual striving after salvation and goodness, with the church as our social centre. Certainly when our leaders make radical statements about public affairs, they do not speak for the majority of churchgoers. Have all these efforts, for example, resulted in any considerable number of Christians taking a more active part in trade union affairs? Of course we do not know, but what evidence we have, suggests not. The Communists continue to exercise an influence in trades union out of all proportion to their numbers by assiduous, active attendance at meetings. Yet there are far more people in this country sympathetic to a Christian view of life than there are members of the Communist Party. But not to anything like the same extent do they make their presence felt in trade union affairs. The churches play an invaluable supportive role in our country, helping many hard-pressed individuals; they also provide a community to belong to for those who believe the gospel. But churchgoers are not conspicuous for their activity in the political field. In some instances, pre-occupation with church affairs takes some good men out of the political struggle. In a few cases, the choice is deliberate. They say that "politics is a dirty business" in which they have no desire to be involved.

In a curious way, the political activity of our leaders can be counter-productive for the rest of us by creating the illusion of involvement without much of the reality. *Apartheid in South Africa?* — that has been dealt with in a recent statement of Philip Potter. *Homelessness of many young people in Britain?* — Did not the Archbishop of Canterbury say something about that the other day?

Thus the commitment of our leaders on issues may absolve us from any responsibility for them. There is a parallel in the mass-media coverage of the news which also creates the illusion of involvement with little of the reality. (When on the television screen we see pictures of starving children in Ethiopia, it is a shock and we may think that this means we are somehow sharing their suffering. Of course it means nothing of the kind. Perversely, watching the suffering of other people can be part of the evening's entertainment. We are in danger of becoming a nation of voyeurs, not viewers.)

The fact is that most Christians today are working with a model of the church as an ark not an army. And a very good ark it is too for those who can clamber aboard. It offers shelter against the storms that are raging outside. Here we have one of the best chances today of being recognized as unique individuals of infinite value, however discouraged we may be in the world; here is one spot on earth where we may well know everybody else and are encouraged to believe that everybody is interested in us. For most of us the church is a centre for rest and recuperation, not a place for a briefing session or an advanced post well within enemy lines. All the writings and activities of politically-minded church leaders have not substantially changed the image. "All the king's horses and all the king's men" have not been able to provide political experiences at local level as an integral part of the Christian way of life. There are many reasons for this relative failure. Chief among them clearly is the immensity of the task. But we cannot overlook or entirely forgive a defective communication. Some of the literature on the subject is written in a style which suggests that it is directed towards an educated elite: as though one needed at least two "A" levels to be a Christian activist.

Not unkindly, I hope, I wish to spell out in more detail what it means to say that the average churchgoer sees the church as an ark rather than an army with a mission. And let me admit at once that the features I am about to deplore as inhibiting "Christian activism", I find to a degree within myself when I join in acts of public worship.

(i) *Churchgoers are looking primarily for the satisfaction of their own emotional needs.* These are real, of course, and must be met. We are unlikely to continue our membership of any organization which does nothing to satisfy our basic emotional needs. So in church we may hope that our moral and spiritual batteries are re-charged; that we are encouraged to start again despite our previous failures; that we correct our standards and realize we matter, at least to God, and that this whole world has not strayed beyond his love and care. All this is fine and necessary. But if it is allowed to fill the whole picture, it is hard to see how going to church is more than a weekly morale-boosting session. And it misses a feature which may give us the deepest satisfaction. That is to be told that God needs us in his fight against the evil forces that are loose in our world, and to be given some guidance as to what we may do.

When I attend services in various parts of the country, I feel sometimes that they are geared almost exclusively to the satisfaction of immediate emotional needs and that somebody has made the shrewd if unconscious decision, that if this is not so, we cannot retain the support of our people. "Far, far away, like bells at even pealing,/The voice of Jesus sounds o'er land and sea", happily sings the congregation. The words are designed to lull us into a false sense of security. But if God is at the heart of our struggle, and Christ is a contemporary figure, then his voice is uncomfortably near. I feel this particularly in what have come to be called "Family Church Services". Of course, the original intention was worthy. It was a necessary development of the experimental approach in religious education with its stress on the development of the individual: it added the dimension of the church as a community. But see what all too commonly has happened to the aspiration. A large number of children make a token appearance at the worship — they may only be there for eleven minutes. They may in fact not hear the Scriptures read or join in saying the Lord's Prayer with the rest of the congregation; then the preacher, who has been fighting with the hosts of the Lord suddenly finds himself struggling with the righteous remnant. Even more serious is the pre-occupation with communication to the neglect of content. Everything must be made simple and entertaining — everything is an aspect of show business. (Movements which have nothing left to say begin to concentrate on how to say it). The result is that acts of public worship resemble a light entertainment performance. Morning worship begins to look like an ecclesiastical multi-coloured swap-shop.

(ii) *Our associations with churches are often strongly tinged — whether we know it or not — with nostalgia.* Oh, for the sight of a vanished age when the world was so much better and simpler, when we ourselves were younger and further from the end! (In a Kung phrase, we dust the paper flowers when we should be growing roses.)[7] Again it is only the distortion of this demand that is to be deplored. It is right to go to church to look for something that never changes in this changing world. "Oh safe to the Rock that is higher than I", is a respectable cry. Some of the translations of German hymns by John Wesley anticipate features of Jung's psychology with its emphasis on security. "Fixed on this ground will I remain." Bewildered by the pace of change, we properly look in church for the immutable, but it is possible to allow this demand to be too prominent, to carry it to neurotic levels.

In the Bible, we find God constantly offering men adventure rather than security. He is always telling them to strike camp and push on. Obstinately and nervously, they may cling to the known and familiar, but some like Abraham go out not knowing whither they go. The disciples found Jesus a disturbing figure because he was always for moving on just when they felt safe and settled. And Christians today should think of Christ not as any longer nailed to a cross but as striding ahead into new adventures and inviting us to go with him. Christians are confronted with a recurring paradox. Christ is both unchanging and changing. "Jesus Christ is the same yesterday, today and for ever" (Hebrews 13:8, NEB.) But Christ speaks a distinctive word to each generation. And each age has its own image of him. In the early centuries, he was Christ the king; in the Middle Ages he was the Christ of suffering. Our picture of Christ is partly fashioned by the circumstances of our times; but it is also because his personality is so rich and varied that succeeding ages keep discovering new facets of his saving grace. We have to ask "Who is Jesus for us today?" as well as appreciating what he was for ages past. In a sense, their picture is no use to us. Every generation has to discover Christ for itself, because every generation has its own tasks, its own "challenge and response", in the Toynbee model. "Who is Jesus for us?" And somehow I do not think the answer is, "Our ultimate security who guarantees the ancient certainties." The answer has more to do with One who inspires community in this world where science has annihilated distance and which has become in consequence a global village.

(iii) There is a third factor which hinders attempts to include political involvement as part of the life-style of local and non-professional Christians. *Church-going operates to turn us into "locals" rather than "cosmopolitans".* The terms of course are taken from Margaret Stacey's classic sociological study of Banbury.[8] Here she describes two kinds of people, the "locals" and the "cosmopolitans". There were the older families steeped in the tradition of Banbury, whose interest was mainly in the town, the countryside around and the local inhabitants. They seemed to know everybody and the activities of the local people interested them far more than, say, the journeys of the American Secretary of State. By contrast, the "cosmopolitans" were the newcomers whose interests extended far beyond Banbury to the whole world. (Under modern conditions, the "locals" will survive only in rural areas and small towns, and even there their attitudes will be affected by the world coverage of news, daily piped into every home.) In the summer of 1977, I visited Ilkley, a small town in the West Riding of Yorkshire. During my stay, world events as usual shattered our peace. President Carter had to make a decision about whether to put funds into the development of the neutron bomb, which some suppose to be tactically superior because it kills people and leaves property undamaged. And fighting had broken out at last between the Egyptians and the Libyans. As I walked down the main street, I noticed that outside the news-agent's shops, only the poster for the local paper gave any indication of the contents. It announced: "Town Hall puts up charges for rent of rooms." The editor understood that his readers looked to him for local rather than world news.

Now it is the fashion to scorn the "locals". Have they not heard that due to technology we are all neighbours now?; that what happens in any part of the world may affect everybody else in every part of the world; that "peace is indivisible", in the famous phrase of Litvinov?; that no no human group is likely to survive in isolation from the rest?

But I do not want to state the issue in these simple "either-or" terms. It seems to me that the future belongs to those who can relate in loyalty and identification both to the local community and the world community. It is possible to use the cosmopolitan challenge to evade the local challenge; to be active in support of the poor in Calcutta partly as an excuse for not wanting to do anything about those unpleasant people next door. Charles Dickens was able to caricature this "remote charity" better than any other writer. Several of his characters combine lack of charity to their immediate neighbours with a passion to help people in distant lands. In *Bleak House* he describes Mrs. Jellyby who was devoted to the improvement of African people, but neglectful of her own family. No wonder that the long-suffering Mr. Jellyby said to his children, "Never have a mission, my dear children."

Parish pump politics are not just insular: they are important. If we cannot love the neighbour whom we can see and touch how can we possibly love the neighbour who is too far away to see and touch?

My present grumble is that too much of our church life favours insularity, weights the scales on the side of local interest. If ideally we seek to be both local citizens and world citizens, far too much attention is devoted to the former. It is not true, of course, that churches and chapels ignore the world situation. There are sacrificial efforts to support missionary work; and there is literature on world affairs (though mostly about the world church) scattered around most churches. And,

not least, there are intercessory prayers for the world, its problems and trouble-spots. All this however may suffer from the
defect previously identified as the illusion of involvement with
little of the reality. Intercessory prayers are one example of this
defect. Splendid in intention, they may be disturbing in practice, simply satisfying our own need to feel that we are doing
something about a situation that is quite intolerable. Recently I
was present at a service when the preacher wandered up and
down the aisle inviting the congregation to make suggestions for
intercessory prayers. "India", said one worshipper. "Yes",
eagerly responded the preacher, "let us pray for the people of
India." And that was all. There are at least 500 million in India.
How realistic was the prayer? If we pray for a member of the
congregation who is ill, we can send him flowers or a message of
cheer. Intercessory prayers with no possibility of action may be
psychologically dangerous for us since they arouse feelings of
compassion for which there is no expression. Almost certainly,
intercessory prayers of this vague nature satisfy our own need
"to do something about it". In this particular case, the prayer
for India was offered at a time (1977) when a fund had been set
up to help the victims of a cyclone in that sub-continent, but no
reference was made to this enterprise. If intercessory prayers are
offered for "Third World" countries, the church's educational
programmes have to include some information about those
countries. If we are to pray for the nations and groups we must
be helped to see the contemporary world as an arena for the
saving activity of God.

(iv) There is yet one more inhibiting factor. *Politics is known
to include a strong element of controversy and so can be
divisive, splitting families, fellowship and friendship groups.
And this conflicts with a common image of the church as a
happy band of people who get along well with each other and do
not indulge in argument.* So there is a strong disposition to keep
"politics" out of church life. A leading divine once said to me,
"If there is anything in this class conflict, I hope we shall not
talk about it too much in the churches". We have boasted about
being non-political when we ought really to aim at being multi-
political. In commending their church to "outsiders", people
will award it the highest accolade as being "happy — we all have
a good time there".

Christians are tempted to pretend that the world is other than it is and in particular to ignore its conflicts; or they may tend to make the church an oasis of camaraderie in the midst of a desert war. Of course, there is no merit in controversy for its own sake, and there is a profound sense in which a church should be a happy place and a haven from the storm that is raging outside. But only by accepting, not evading, necessary controversy. Christians above all men should be able to argue without quarelling, bringing their political differences into church life and still being united in Christ. There is no more relevant scene today than a Tory councillor and a member of the Tribune Group kneeling side by side at the communion rail. Christians have something worth arguing about. We shall have to examine the present image of the church as a "non-controversial" community before we can begin to see political activity as part of the life-style of local congregations.

And — to stress again the underlying theme of this section — it is to the local congregation that we must look for the next great stride in the political education of Christians. We want local leaders who can give a localized and educational expression to the great vision that has come to world-leaders of the Church: that God is at the heart of contemporary struggles for justice, peace and freedom; that the ritual of the church is not a separate theatre remote from the central issues of our time; and that a new and exciting, if perplexing, dimension can be added to discipleship today. It is to local leaders that we must look to provide political involvement as part of the staple diet of Christian obedience.

It is unnecessary to over-state the case. The primary purpose of the Church is the worship of God (though if the Bible is to be believed, he is a "political God" deeply involved in current affairs). Christians are involved in twin paradoxes. In a world like this — tragic, threatened, with much immemorial pain and injustice — they continually celebrate a victory over evil won by Christ. Amidst global dilemmas, they exhibit their belief in the importance of individual development and fulfilment. Moreover, the local ministers have to take account of the expectations of their congregations, not straying too far from the unwritten contract between them and their people. They are prophets as well as pastors, called to lead the people into the purposes of God, and not merely to mirror their expectations.

A local church which tries to ignore the political dimension of our lives serves its members ill. It issues moral exhortations in a vacuum. Churches may generate a power which is always in neutral gear, never engaged with some of the major moral tasks of our time. To change the figure — they involve us in shadow-boxing, not in a real fight.

It looks a more hopeful strategy to devote our main efforts to the political education of the young. One is driven to the conclusion that the pietistic and individualistic attitudes of many older Christians are so deeply entrenched, that it is doubtful whether they can now be changed. Treacherously perhaps, one is tempted to repeat the question that Nicodemus asked: "But how is it possible for a man to be born when he is old?" (John 3:4, NEB).

2
The Political Education of the Young in Britain

The Movement

For more than a decade now there has been a lobby to promote the political education of the young, in schools and in other branches of educational provision. It is supported by powerful and persuasive advocates like Professor Bernard Crick and Derek Heater. A small library of books has been written on the subject. Several research enterprises have been mounted including the Schools Council support for the *Programmes for Political Education 13-19* project.

There is a research unit at York University funded by the Nuffield Trust. Starting in April 1975, the B.B.C. (Radio 3) devoted eight programmes to the subject. The Hansard Society has produced valuable papers which seek to explore the subject in depth yet still to offer practical suggestions for curricula. The argument has reached traditional voluntary youth organizations. The Scouts for example have set up a committee one of whose tasks is to explore the possibilities of political education in their units.

But until recently, the movement had not attracted public interest and support. Nor had the Department of Education and Science spoken unambiguously on the subject. It remained on the drawing boards of a few experts and enthusiasts. But in 1977 the situation changed swiftly and dramatically. Two inspectors wrote a report in favour of political education in the schools. At the time, the Minister of Education (Mrs. Shirley Williams) and the former Opposition spokesman (Mr. Norman St. John Stevas) were in favour of the idea. And the public began to show at least a mild interest. The present position is that there is

wide agreement that political education within the educational
system should be attempted. Doubts remain as to its form, content and intention.

The main reason for this quickening of concern and shift of
direction is certain events connected mainly with the activities of
the National Front in 1977. (Threatening events prompt educational change more speedily than educational theories.) The
National Front set out to recruit a youth movement. They dis-
tributed their periodical *Bulldog* among school pupils. In a
television interview, one of their organizers said they hoped to
re-cycle some of the aggressiveness of football hooligans and
vandals. The reaction to all this was immediate and strong. An
attempt by the National Front to hold a youth rally in Birmingham on February 18th, 1977, led to violent clashes with the
police. Linked with this fear was a contrary one, that in the
classroom and lecture room students were likely to receive
indoctrination from the opposite camp — the Marxist.
Professor Goulding reported that many lecturers in higher
education advocated an uncritical acceptance of the ideology of
the Left. Thoughtful observers posed the question another way.
"If social democracy is the attempt to maximize both economic
justice and personal freedom, can such systems survive unless
they offer programmes of political education to their young
people, and seek to gain their support for a way of life which
seems right?"

Some of the opposition to the notion of political education
crumbled when it was understood that the young were to be
politically educated (or indoctrinated) anyway, either from the
extreme Right or the extreme Left. Suddenly it was widely
realized that it was an urgent matter for the country to offer to
the young forms of political education which were presumed to
be right. But the enthusiasts are not home yet. Many people see
dangers and difficulties in this development.

There are several formidable obstacles. One is the shortage of
political educators and so far as I know there is no college of
education which offers this kind of training to its students.
Another difficulty is the confusion which arises because the
words used in discussion do not always carry the same meaning
for the different people using them. There is, for example, an
outrageous ambiguity about the use of the very word
"politics". Sometimes it has an "idealism" connotation, as

when Professor Bernard Crick says that politics is the public action of free men.[1] But there is the opposite and derogatory meaning, so that to call a man a politician may be the equivalent of swearing at him, as when an M.P. will accuse one of his opponents of "acting politically" or being "politically motivated". This ambiguity bedevils the whole enterprise and will be the subject later of more detailed and careful consideration.

Lack of interest in the subject

One daunting prospect confronts the exponents of programmes of political education for the young, namely the lack of interest in the subject by large sections of the youth population. The serious decline in the membership of the youth wings of the major political parties over the past few decades is only one indication of this phenomenon. Most young people are happily pre-occupied with growing up, looking for a bit of excitement and working for their futures. A glazed look comes over their eyes if anybody introduces the subject of politics which they regard as boring and beyond their comprehension. It is instructive to consider the two political movements which in our time have attracted the spontaneous support of large numbers of young people. One was the Campaign for Nuclear Disarmament which enjoyed its heyday in the late 50s and early 60s. The other is the fastest-growing political movement in contemporary Britain (1978) — the Anti-Nazi League, whose avowed object is to oppose the activities of the National Front. (In the first year of its history, 208 local branches were established: at a carnival organized by the League on September 24th, 1978, 100,000 people were present.) There are weaknesses in both movements. They are vulnerable to internal dissension and waning enthusiasm. They are likely to be used by infiltrating Marxists who will manipulate the movement to gain support for their own ideology. The hopes of some of the members may be naive. But at least at one single point they have something to teach enthusiasts for political education in that they have succeeded in winning the support of some young people who previously had shown no disposition to be politically active. The main reasons are obvious. They simplify politics to one issue which calls for action. Moreover, as the fight is against injustice to a section of the population, they appeal to the idealism of young people. No doubt also, some of these youthful participants gain a feeling of personal significance from their activities; because they are needed to fight in a worthy cause.

Here are guidelines for us. Programmmes of political education for the young should include large elements of "something to do". Racism is not the only evil in our society. Many young people in this country suffer from deprivation and neglect by their own community, and there are issues which touch them closely — like youth unemployment and lack of grant-aided educational opportunities. Some endure injustice at the hands of the authorities: there is, for example, a *prima facie* case for examining whether some police officers, in the exercise of their immensely difficult task, have not been guilty of discrimination against some young blacks. There are groups of young people aggressive on this account who thus become examples of the oft-quoted threat to law and order. Political education and constitutional action would not be a further threat. Fortunately, the alternative to alienation is not quiescence but responsible political activity for our own sake, and subsequently on behalf of others. This is where many will begin their political involvement, with their own grievances. Not everybody is a born and bred liberal. In this activity, some of them will 'come of age' and gain personal significance. They will not forever be unaware of the fact that we now live in a community where social groups — small traders as well as factory workers — must organize themselves to act politically if they are to obtain their rights. Critics will argue with force, that the politicization of the young will lead to a further fragmentation of our society into warring groups each intent on their own interests and with no concern for the common good. But such critics are probably pining for the old days that will never return when there were established and unquestioned structures of authority. Moreover, it is unlikely that they have met many of the disgruntled youngsters known to youth workers. These carry a grudge against their society and all authority figures: in extreme cases, they are atavistic, striking out in all directions, feeling they have been seriously let down, not finding love and care where they expected both. Even relatively well-provided youngsters often feel frustrated by their powerlessness in the face of huge institutions which decide their fate. Research has revealed that many of them would like to have more power even if they did not use it. Political education (in one aspect) is an optimistic attempt to persuade some of these people to re-cycle their aggression and resentment in the form of responsible political action.

But what of the obstacle which arises from the fact that many young people find modern politics too complicated to understand? That was the reply given by 52% of the interviewees in the Stradling enquiry.[2] Apart from the stress on action, already identified, this seems to be a challenge to the educator rather than an insurmountable barrier. Let us take for example one of the most significant political discussions being carried on in this country at the present time and one which engaged in debate intellectual high-flyers like Mr. Roy Hattersley and Sir Keith Joseph. It concerns the meaning of the word "equality" as a goal for a civilized community. What do we intend when we say that we want people to be "equal"? Equal in wealth? Equal at law? Equal in opportunity? Whatever the final outcome of this debate, it should be possible for a good teacher — eshewing the language of Hattersley and Joseph — to make this matter intelligible to a thirteen-year-old of average ability, not merely by supplying living exmples of the different interpretations, but by relating the issue to the youngster's own experience, prospects and opportunities.

It is to Professor Bernard Crick that we owe the most useful suggestions in this area.[3] Not only does he insist that any teaching about politics should begin with specific issues and only then introduce general concepts, but he gives lively examples of how political education can be rooted in the day-to-day experience of the youngster. Thus, when he says the referee's decision was "not fair", he may be initiating a discussion which explores the meaning of "Justice". Our deepest need at the moment, in this area, is for educators who — without becoming bores — can help young people to explore the political implications of their common experiences.

Can political education be distinguished from political indoctrination?

But there is one misgiving which over-shadows all the rest. Politics in our society has become so much a matter of partisanship, of commitment to a party or an ideology, that it is thought not to be possible to teach it without bias; "political education" must surely prove in practice to be "political indoctrination". Understandably many people shrink from the prospect. They have a picture of what happens in monolithic totalitarian states where political education means the communication of one point of view which cannot be questioned. And they think that this will not only be a severe restriction upon the freedom of the students, but is also alien to the liberal tradition in the British educational system. These critics may turn to an attractive alternative. Admitting the need for some form of political education, they want to drain the subject of all controversy and make it into "civics" or "preparation for citizenship". They are ready to talk about the structures and processes of politics but say nothing about its conflicting ideas and practice. They aim to keep controversy out of the classroom and the lecture-room. It may be questioned whether the educational institutions can be so pure-minded and remote as to ignore the controversies that are raging in a pluralistic society. Can they any longer operate with a consensus model of social integration and ignore the conflict?

It has to be admitted that the teacher who opts for political education is likely to have some bias or prejudice of his own in this area. The same of course can be said of the religious educator. It may be that both of them may be better teachers because they have their own commitment. Perhaps rootless people plant few trees. But of course this bias will tempt them "to cook the evidence".[4] This may not be a conscious process. Our preferences are part of our personality and we do not exist apart from them. We cannot shed them like an overcoat on a warm afternoon. Both religion and politics belong to a wide range of subjects, where we do not usually find facts unrelated to their interpretations. And both subjects are "value-loaded" in the sense that they call for a commitment. What then? Are we to say that only people without political commitments can be good political educators? Not so, but we have a right to ask that they be undogmatic, fair-minded, open-minded: in fact that they be educators rather than propagandists: seeking critical examination rather than unthinking commitment, being teachers not recruiting sergeants, assailed by doubts about their own conclusions, and certainly not persuaded that they have received the final and absolute truth. Above all, they should be ready openly to admit their own bias so that this may be taken into account by the student and assessed. For years, as a lecturer, I sedulously avoided any reference in the lecture-room or the seminar to my own value-preference, both political and religious, supposing that to be "value-free" in this way was to be fair-minded and professional. One day a student pointed out to me that it would be more respectful to the students to declare my own position at some point and so allow them to take account of my unconscious bias. I saw the point and mended my ways.

Moreover, there is a sense in which education is always political. As Illich has pointed out, it must assume an ideology and take place within a context of assumed values. To suppose otherwise is to make the same mistake as those who think that scientific investigation proceeds by collecting facts without a theory.

But of course, in over a century and more of popular education, it is clear what has been the main political thrust. Schools have supported the establishment. Socialization there has been a process to persuade the youngsters to accept their society's values, conform, and never to question or seek to change any of them. We do not have to go back to Hannah More to find examples. A contemporary writer, Laurie Lee, describes his own school. "Unhearing, unquestioning, we rocked to our chanting, hammering the gold nails home. 'Twice-two are four.' 'One-God-is-love.' 'One-Lord is king.' 'One-king-is-George.' So it always was, had been, would be for ever: we asked no questions: we didn't hear what we said: yet neither did we ever forget."[5] Further back, in 1868, there is the characteristic Taunton Committee Report dominated by class consciousness and wishing to base thereon a system of secondary education which would reinforce the structure.

The point being made is that the present plea is not to *start* political education since it has always been there. The present hope is that it can be *improved* partly by bringing it into the open. The process is less likely to be indoctrinating and propagandist if it is avowed and examinable. Nor should it be only a persuasion to support the existing system but contain an invitation to young poeple to join in efforts to transform their society where this is called for. Of course, there is the danger — frequently pointed out — that the pendulum might swing too far the other way and that an imposed ideology of the Establish-

ment might be replaced by an imposed ideology of the Left.
That would be equally wrong. We cannot allow people to use
the democratic machinery to destroy the democratic process.
What we want in the classroom is not an ideology, but
ideologies to be exposed to scrutiny.

The need today

Events connected with the activities of the National Front
may be said, then, to have added considerable momentum to
the movement for political education. But beyond these
happenings are other reasons of longer standing.

One is that politics and political decisions play an increasing
part in the life of the individual citizen. This is a reflection of the
fact that government — both central and local — intervenes
more and more in our lives. This process, beginning in 1914, has
reached its apex in our generation. The laissez-faire doctrines of
Adam Smith (1723-90) gave rise to the notion that the best
government was that which interfered least in the affairs of the
nation. This approach has become less plausible with the passing of time. The advance of technology alone demands that
political decisions must be made by government, decisions
which affect us all. Citizens require a measure of political
literacy to understand what is being done to them. But paradoxically, they are called upon to make more political decisions.
Politicians are still, to a marked and perhaps even increasing
degree, at the mercy of public opinion. It may well be that in the
coming years we shall see more and more use being made of the
referendum as an instrument of political decision.

Moreover, there is a growing demand today for what is called
"a participative democracy" in which citizens have a bigger part
in the decision-making which affects their lives, where power is
spread more widely throughout the land. This is in contrast with
"the elective democracy" following the nineteenth century
model of Mill where, almost exclusively, citizens exercise their
democratic rights through the ballot-box and hand over the
decision-making to their representatives. "Bureaucracy" has
become a dirty word in twentieth century Britain. Books like
Popper's *The Open Society and its Enemies* have had a wide
influence even amongst those who have never read them. The
spread of political power is connected with "Community
Development", a movement which so far has promised more

than it has been able to deliver. But its hope relies upon higher levels of political literacy among our population: if we are to act politically we need political education.

All of this of course relates with particular force to the young people of Britain. As in most societies, they are a source of perennial interest and concern. The young are usually seen both as a threat and a promise. They are a threat because, as Mannheim suggested, having less stake in the established order of things, they are more likely to sink the boat. They are a promise, because they represent not only the true wealth of the nation, but they are also the hope that the nation will persist into the future with a recognizable identity.

We often talk today — and not quite accurately — of "the problem of youth". This is often followed by hand-wringing exercises. In so far as the phrase has any meaning it refers to the anti-social and self-destructive activities of a not insignificant minority of the younger generation. Perhaps we ought to be more worried by the lack of social interest among a larger number. (In this respect of course they do not differ materially from older people.) For what lies at the basis of both attitudes is an alienation from society: they do not feel involved, they do not feel that they belong to Britain and Britain belongs to them. Fanatical devotion to a particular football team is probably a surrogate sense of belonging in a society which does not provide it.

If alienation is the deepest "disease" then the most radical cure is the long-term offer of partnership across the generations in pursuit of moral goals. And it is this which is lacking today. In 1960, the Albermarle Report[6] said: "There does not seem to be at the heart of our society a courageous and exciting struggle for a particular moral and spiritual life — only a passive, neutral commitment to things as they are". Nearly twenty years on, can anybody say that the situation is different? But if it is to be changed there is at least one essential element, namely the offer to the young of programmes of political education, and the offer of political involvement and action in the pursuit of a decent community. Society needs the idealism and energy and ideas of the young. The young need to feel that society needs them.

What is politics?
The point has already been made that progress is inhibited by

the ambiguity of the terms used. Any rational discussion of the
subject is made difficult by the changing mental image brought
on by the word "politics". Ask any six people to write down
their definition and you may receive six different answers. It is
time to look at some of the popular images and to offer a
definition which will be used as the basis of the present exploration.

The mass media tend to project politics as a clash of personalities, mainly because of a vested interest in dramatizing the
news. This has been shown to be good for circulation and
audience ratings. To personalize the news is not only to
dramatize it, to make it an aspect of show-business, it is also to
simplify it for popular consumption, though doing so
frequently over-simplifies the issues. Of course, the personalities of the chief actors is part of the stuff of politics: character
will affect choices, preferences, decisions. But not to anything
like the degree that the mass media pretend. Politicians are
confronted by inalienable facts and their freedom to manoeuvre
is usually greatly exaggerated. Certainly the scope for their
individual character traits is limited. The unflappability of Mr.
MacMillan, the avuncular charm of Mr. Callaghan, the iron
resolve of Mrs. Thatcher — all these — and much more, make
good theatre. But they are not decisive in terms of political
direction.

Strongly contrasted are the comparative few for whom
politics is primarily a matter of principles. The philosopher-
kings who deal in the ideas of a subject, they are in danger of
becoming gurus, removed from the arena where politics is
mainly about power. They sometimes naively assume that men
engage in the political struggle to forward ideals rather than to
forward their own interests and satisfy their own needs. That is
why this group is often heavily criticized by the Marxists who in
this matter are far more realistic and view such philosophers as a
bourgeois élite who can afford to be high-souled.

The next group differs materially from the last. They see
politics primarily as something to be achieved and therefore in
terms of three affiliated realities — power, party and propaganda. It is action rather than ideas and the dogmas are not to
be questioned.

All three groups display one serious flaw. They are disposed
to see politics as existing only in our political institutions —

Parliament, the parties, the local council. Whereas it is the present contention that politics is a fact of everyday life *outside* these institutions: it is expressed in the family, the school, the youth club and so on.

This will become clear with a new definition. One of the most satisfying descriptions is to be found in Discussion Document No. 5 issued in April 1976 by the Hansard Society: "Throughout this paper we have used the word 'politics' to refer to the process through which conflicts of interests and values within a group are conciliated. Such conflicts generally arise over the way in which scarce resources are allocated, and by resources we mean not only material goods but also power, status, skills, time and space. This kind of conflict can occur in any group of two or more people . . . but does not necessarily lead to political activity. Recourse to this process of conciliation is most likely to occur in those groups where there is some element of compulsion upon the members which makes secession from the group difficult, and therefore conciliation is necessary if the group is to continue to exist. The most obvious example of such a group is the State which, through its territorial monopoly of legitimate authority, is able to use such sanctions as the power over life and death, imprisonment and exile in attempts to enforce its decision. Other groups may not have such weighty sanctions but are still characterized by some element of compulsory membership, e.g. the school. Political activity is not so frequent or so exclusive in voluntary groups. The absence of compulsion means that when there is a serious conflict of interest or values the group may simply break up. There is, then, a qualitative difference between voluntary and involuntary groups which should be borne in mind when looking at the politics of everyday life."

The paper then goes on to state that political activity is initiated when people feel they are affected unfairly by decisions that have been made, and moreover, that these decisions are not inevitable but may be changed. The political activity taken will be guided by four considerations: *Goals:* what are we trying to achieve, what purpose will a given action serve? *Values:* in what ways would it be right to act? *Methods:* how should we do it? *Results:* was it the right outcome? the fairest? the best? the one that was required?

The politics of everyday life might be illustrated from the

familiar situation where there are repeated conflicts between parents and adolescent children as to which television programmes to watch. It is an issue about the shared use of a scarce resource. The children may feel that they are being denied their rights by the parents' unjust use of their status, authority and power. They combine in order to change the situation. They want to gain more of their own choices (goals); they must do this without too flagrant a challenge to Dad's authority and position (values); several suggestions are put forward, one being to save up enough money to buy a portable television set (methods); if they adopted this solution, how has it worked out? — Has it led to a deeper rift in the family (results)?

Many more illustrations could be quoted. A youth club housed in a school is denied the use of facilities by the headmaster who claims that the decision is his and his alone. The youth leader and his colleagues feel they must take some action. In a college of education, the students request a course of philosophy but their request is turned down — on the grounds of the shortage of teaching resources — by the academic board, mostly composed of tutors. What are the students to do now? They have to plan political action with the same principles involved as in the case of the family disputing about the use of the television set. A comparable situation arises in a school where, say, the headmaster wants to make rules about the dress of pupils.

Politics, then, is what happens in any human organization when there is dispute about the use of limited resources, power, authority and status. The reaction to a felt injustice and the conviction that this may be changed is political activity. This definition can apply to a state, city, town, village, family, school, college, youth club — in fact in any social group where human beings regularly associate, where rules have to be observed, and decisions made. If this is the meaning of politics, the broad river has three tributaries:

(a) Structures — parliament, political parties, councils, committees, appointment of officers, family consultations.

(b) Processes — what form the political activity takes, such as the work of elected representatives, elections, public enquiries, appeal committees, pressure group activity.

(c) Ideas — political activity is guided by our personal

philosophy (what we think is important, to which goals we would give priority) and this of course explains many of our political differences. An Israeli "sees" a different Middle East situation from a member of the P.L.O. At home, a Tory gives high priority to personal and political freedom; a Marxist may seek economic justice above all else. One major area of difference is between those who want to use politics for change and those who see it primarily as a means of preserving stability, and law and order.

What is political education?

Again we are confronted by the conflicting answers given to this question. For some, it is almost entirely concerned with the acquisition of skill, learning how "to work the system", to gain advantages for yourself and your group. Others, by contrast, see political education as an academic subject, the communication of knowledge. For the first it is primarily about power and for the second about ideas.

The present view is that neither of these two extremes represents the correct starting place. For many young people in our country, political literacy will begin with the appreciation that politics is a fact of life, part of their daily experience. Our programmes should encourage an awareness of the political dimension of human experience, an understanding that political decisions are being taken all the time that affect our prosperity, welfare and happiness, and that — to repeat a point — political decisions are taken not only in Parliament and local councils but in homes and schools. We should try to understand politics better simply because "it is there".

Broadly speaking, education is a process by which we become aware of and respond positively to more and more of our environment. A completely uneducated person would be one whose entire world was restricted to himself. If politics is part of our environment, as are the flowers and the hills, and Mozart's music and Shakespeare's plays, then it is the function of education to help us to be aware of the fact. There is an interesting parallel here with the development of religious education. It used to be thought of as little more than the acquisition of agreed dogmas and doctrines. Then there came the experiential approach which virtually said, "God is not only in the Bible: he is in your present experience. Closer is he than breathing, nearer than hands and feet.'' Similarly, political education should begin by helping young people to interpret and make sense of their present experiences.

This awareness is easy and indeed inevitable, in those many conflict situations which might be called the flash-points of contemporary history. That politics is a part of their lives does not need to be brought to the attention of young people living in Northern Ireland, Berlin, Cyprus, or Israel: it is inescapable, a part of their daily diet. This is not so obvious in relatively stable countries like England but, as we have seen, the politics of everyday life is a reality for us too. But the educator has to find ways of convincingly calling attention to it. For although politics is in the air we breathe, affecting our daily experience — the school we attend, the house we live in, the job opportunities we have, the peace of our world — yet we may not think about it, just as we may never think about the oxygen we are constantly breathing into our lungs. In one sense, politics has been the most neglected subject in our British education system. Take only one illustration from many that clamour for mention. Comenius (1592-1670) was an educational reformer with many ideas about methods and egalitarianism in education which would be widely accepted today. But in his own time he met with strong opposition and spent most of his life in exile. One principal reason was that, whatever the merits of his ideals, they could not flourish in the ideological and political climate of his century. So educational change is affected by politics! But in how many colleges of education is this explained when students come to Comenius in the history of education? The political dimension of life has been neglected in our educational system; at the lower level, this has been part of an ''establishment'' ploy; at the higher level, a fear of indoctrination.

What is political education? Who is politically literate? What should be the aim of our programme? In general we may say that this literacy differs from other forms since it implies an ability to act in co-operation with others for agreed ends. It is not the literacy of the study only but of the living situation where decisions are made about the use of limited resources. It is thus a literacy which involves skills of various kinds.

''The main aim of the project is to enhance 'political literacy', by which we mean the knowledge, skills and attitudes needed to make a man or woman informed about politics, able to participate in public life and groups of all kinds, both occupational and voluntary: and to recognize and tolerate diversities of political and social values. A politically literate person should know what the main political disputes are about, what beliefs the main contestants have of them, how they are likely to affect them, how they relate to institutions and he will have a predisposition to try to be politically effective while respecting the sincerity of others. Obviously political literacy is relevant to everyone . . . Nor do we assume that 'political literacy' is best gained by teaching about politics directly. Of particular importance is how political literacy can be advanced through other subjects, for instance, History, English, Geography, Social Studies, Sociology and Economics.'"[7]

Three elements are involved here (cf. Document 2: *Political Literacy* — Hansard Society. The quotations in the following paragraphs are from this source.)

(a) *Knowledge* We need to be informed about the structures, processes and ideas of politics in many forms of human association, mandatory and voluntary, local, national and international. "In each parliament, factory, school and family, active participants need to know some facts about it, where its money comes from, and something of the ways and means in which it works." It will be said that there never was a time when — through newspapers, radio and television — the British public were fed with so much political information. But it tends to be a selection of tit-bits of information that will make a popular presentation. We are not always offered even a simple explanation of the issues which lie behind the immediate events.

(b) *Attitudes* In politics as in many other subjects, there are no facts unconnected with interpretations. None of us — even the most self-consciously value-free — is without a bias which conditions the facts that we see. At least we should admit this to ourselves and to others, and recognize that other people have other values. Yet there should be certain standards for political discussion and action which are common to all. "All values are not equal. Attitudes cannot be ignored . . . it is both proper and possible to try to nurture and strengthen certain procedural values . . . we identified 'freedom, toleration, fairness, respect of truth and for reasoning.' "

(c) *Skills* Political literacy includes "know-how": it is appropriate action as well as right ideas and correct information. "The ultimate test of political literacy lies in creating a proclivity to action, not in achieving more theoretical analysis . . . The politically literate person must be able to devise strategies for influence and achieving change."

All this discussion leaves untouched the vital matter of method, particularly for the voluntary youth group with which we are concerned. Obviously — as in the related subjects of art and religious education — we should aim to provide experiences rather than lectures. But the question of methods is the sole subject of a later chapter.

The political significance of the community development programme

Since the highest aspiration of the community development movement is to enable local communities to define their own needs and organize their resources to meet those needs, it is clearly an invitation to people to act politically. Though the movement has so far produced disappointing results, there are many examples up and down the country of local projects and a whole literature has been developed around the subject. It is notoriously difficult to arrive at an agreed definition of "community", but several meanings may be included by the theorists and practitioners of community development.

(i) *Psychological* Modern conditions of rapid social change bringing mobility, industrialization and urbanization, have destroyed or damaged many of the old community ties which people knew in small and established groups. A modern substitute must be sought through some form of social engineering.

(ii) *Economic* As a country grows richer, the poor become poorer; community development aims at a fairer distribution of the nation's wealth.

(iii) *Moral* A society should accept responsibility for the development, welfare and fulfilment of its citizens, particularly those who are handicapped in any way.

(iv) *Self-help* Rather than charity, people need the information and support to secure for themselves the resources they need. Better to teach a man to fish than to give him a fish.

(v) *Self-government and participation* Communities define their own needs and organize their resources to satisfy those needs. They engage in corporate struggles against injustice and bureaucracy, demanding more say in the decisions which affect their lives. "Community development" represents the latest point in the evolution of social work thinking and practice. Social work began with an emphasis on case-work: moved quickly through a period where small group work skills were stressed: and has moved into an understanding that it may not always be the proper function of the social worker to persuade the "client" to accept and adjust to his social environment. It may be necessary to help him to organize with others in the attempt to change his social environment. Hence the significance of the movement for political education.

3
The distinctive contribution of the Churches to the political education of the young

An earlier chapter describes some of the difficulties which hinder programmes of political education among Christian groups. The churches have a point of reference that is outside this world, having here 'no abiding city'. Political activity is not part of their traditional life-style. But these obstacles should not be allowed to obscure some real advantages they have in this enterprise. Indeed — as will presently be argued — some of their liabilities may turn out to be assets in another sense.

Brief reference can be made to the practical opportunities presented by their situation. The major educational commitment of the churches is in youth service and is composed of thousands of local units who meet voluntarily each week. There are several reasons why an informal youth service is a better vehicle for political education than the more formal schools' system. Among them are the higher age grouping, the possibility of projects outside the premises, the voluntary nature of the association and the less structured relationship between adults and adolescents. In the church, youth workers usually find themselves confronted not by large classes, but by small groups or individuals, where they can personalize their offering and engage in a two-way system of communication. This was demonstrated in the practice of a Liverpool Salvation Army Captain. He described to me his efforts to help his members to understand better, through group discussion, the world in which they live. Many youngsters today have only a limited vocabulary and teachers and youth workers are constantly using words whose meaning is not clear to them. But this group had developed a ritual for dealing with the situation. Whenever in the discussion anybody heard a word he did not understand, he called out "Marmalade!" and the speaker had to say what the word meant. Those young people would be unlikely to have the confidence to make the same intervention in the classroom and the mass media offer very few opportunities to demand an explanation. The informal atmosphere of the small voluntary group, common in Christian youth work, can be a good vehicle for political as for other forms of education.

But other advantages of the church situation lie at a deeper level.

Not an obsession

The danger of acquiring a political interest is that it may become a political obsession. One has seen this sad result again and again both in teachers and taught. Once we begin to look at the world through political spectacles, then we may start to see not human beings, but "men as trees walking". Politics becomes the "pearl of great price" and we have no eyes for what we regard as lesser pearls.

Obsessive concern with any subject can lead us to de-value our fellows, because we judge them only in the light of their interest and abilities in that subject. We become more interested in the subject than in people, task-related rather than peson-orientated. We still have in many branches of Youth Service people who are called "instructors" (particularly in clubs attached to schools). They are responsible for holding classes (with a voluntary membership) in art, photography, drama or other subjects. Now it is possible to observe three different kinds of instructors; each has a subject and works with people, but they have contrasting methods and attitudes.

(a) *The elitists* are looking for high flyers in the subject; they seek out and encourage the most gifted and may have little interest in the others. Motto: "Train the best and shoot the rest." (The "elitists" are first cousins of the "manipulators" who are interested in controlling the minds of the young for their own ends. Commercial providers are the most frequently-quoted examples, but some Christians have also been in "the youth business" with the same intention.)

(b) *The democrats* are moved by the conviction that possibilities of participation in their subject are more widely spread among the populace than is commonly supposed. Motto: "there's gold in them thar hills."

(c)   *The humanists,* though interested in the subject, are far more interested in the members of the group as human beings, and hence in their growth and development. Motto: "A man's a man for a' that."

There is clearly a danger that the political educator's enthusiasm for the subject may smother enthusiasm for people. On what grounds can we argue that the church is one of the places where this fatal drift may be avoided or halted? Can the claim be substantiated that in the churches we may combat not only political apathy and despair but also political euphoria and utopianism?

The churches may take politics seriously precisely because their faith forbids them to take it too seriously. That the social and political system under which we live should be just, is an important matter; but there is something even more important of which political justice is a part — that men should be reconciled to God. There is an underlying theme in the Christian understanding of life. It is not, "Politics (or anything else) is all-important": it is, "Everything matters, but nothing matters absolutely." We see life itself as a drama which is endlessly teaching the same lesson rather than an evolutionary process in which the individual is caught up. So the church values old Mrs. Jones up the road, bed-ridden with age and arthritis — though she will never be politically active. And Bill Bairstow thinks it is worthwhile meeting half a dozen difficult lads every week and contributing to their growth and development. The church cares too much for individuals ever to become politically obsessed. That is the answer to those people who fear that the church would be less of a caring community if it became involved in programmes of political education. But it is also the factor which is a check and a balance against too intense a concern with politics. It may well be that those who take politics seriously but not too seriously are likely to be the best political educators.

It is precisely because political activity can never become an obsession for Christians that we who advocate more political participation by believers should listen carefully and courteously to those in the church who disagree with us. What are some of the points they make? One is that the Christian faith includes much celebration. And we happily agree. Christians practise a paradox. In a world like this they constantly celebrate a victory which Christ has won over evil. Our critics also point out that the church gives practical help to those in need whilst displaying little enthusiasm for political theories. Who in the end will be found to have done most for the poor of Calcutta — Mother Teresa and her nuns, or the political planners? Does not the gospel say that the widow gave more with her mite than all the rest, and is this not literally true since her reported deed has inspired acts of charity through nineteen centuries? We do not demur from these propositions. In every association, political action can become a shabby substitute for community caring and individual responsibility. At the end of the discussion we only want to say "Yes . . . but". We believe the gospel tells of a God who cares both for individuals and nations, who is the Shepherd and also the Lord of history. So we look for a church that is both pastorally and politically effective. Those Christians who say they want to preach the gospel but keep out of politics (as for example, some missionaries in Rhodesia) must have Bibles with large sections missing, and notably the eighth century prophets. It is undeniable that the primary function of the church is "spiritual". She is there to preach the gospel, but we must go back to the Bible and ask, "What is the gospel?" Her task is to represent the love of God on the contemporary scene but we ask whether that love includes a desire to free men in this life from tyranny and oppression. She is a visible monument in time to the invisible God, but we ask, "What is that God like?" It is quite true that there are dangers for the church in political involvement, the main one being that she will forget her distinctive message and merely put a gloss on secular hopes and outlook. But there can be no prophetic church without dangers.

Put not your trust in politics

Likewise, Christians may put a brake on the extravagant hopes sometimes entertained by political enthusiasts who may be inclined to see social change as a panacea for all the ills which afflict us. Christians should approach human affairs with a powerful mixture of compassion and realism. They know that political revolution — like scientific humanism — has not been able to deliver all that is promised. In abolishing some ancient wrongs, it has created new injustices, transferring tyrannical power from one group to another.

That is why the deepest misgiving Christians have about Marxists is not that they are "materialistic" but that they are naive. They possess the realism to grasp that there is something quite seriously wrong with the world in its present working but they believe that all can be set right by a change in the system of production and distribution. Having identified the economic basis of society, and exposed the illusion of impartiality, they then proceed to build their own Tower of Babel, as Niebuhr suggests.

Government has of course a major rôle to play in enhancing the quality of life for its citizens. But its potential is not un- limited, and it is vital that we should see its limitations as well as its possibilities in an age when the government of the day inter- venes more and more in the lives of individuals. Good govern- ment can do much to create the minimum conditions under which we can have a better chance of being truly human. It can set an example in moral decisions about things like racism. But it cannot of itself give life. The Christian insight is that only God can give us life; man cannot organize his own fulfilment; and the Kingdom of God will not be realized by social engineer- ing or man-management. It is a frequent delusion of politicians that they have more power than they really possess. Napoleon was told (so the story goes) that there had been a decay in French literature and a renaissance was required. The Emperor replied, "I will speak to the Minister of the Interior about that." But creative genius is not at the beck and call of politicians, however powerful.

A prevalent contemporary delusion is that "if we get the structures of the organization right, new life will follow". This stems from a conceit about our management skills. We forget the corollary: "If we have new life, we can find the appropriate structures." Any form of government is like a pump which can only use the amount of water in the reservoir.

The message of the churches helps believers to gain this insight. They see mankind as needing renewal as well as good government, redemption as well as emancipation, reconciliation to God and their own true nature as well as liberation. Paradox- ically, it is because believers are less likely than others to have illusions about the effects of political education, that they are fitted to be political educators.

Individual goodness as well as social righteousness

The nineteenth-century preachers in this country were addicted to phrases like, "The soul of all improvement is the improvement of the soul." This was linked with aphorisms such as, "You can't carve rotten wood" and "We must get the slums out of the people, not the people out of the slums."

We do not commonly hear such phrases today. For over a century the social scientists have been at work persuading us that personality is largely a product of social environment. Karl Marx showed that the industrial worker is the prisoner of a system that alienates him from his own true nature as a human being. Nobody wants us to go back to the days of Christian individualism and pietism, when, at least unconsciously, the church was a tool of capitalist exploitation.

But it may be asked whether today the pendulum has not swung too far in the opposite direction. One lie does not expunge another. Are we now hoping for too much from collective action and neglecting the factor of individual responsibility? Do we naively suppose that a welfare state is the same as a caring community? We are constantly expecting the state to accept liberal and generous social policies when these are not supported by the moral intentions of individuals, almost as though we think we can have immoral men in a moral society.

The recent Wolfenden Report[1] had many encouraging things to say about voluntary social work and in some senses it is likely to be definitive for the next 25 years. It referred enthusiastically to the large volume of "informal voluntary social" work undertaken by neighbours and family; the hope for the future was that this would grow. But it had no practical suggestions to make for this expansion, confining its attention to the political re-structuring of the organization of voluntary work in this country.

Ideally, the church is not so naive. It knows that only with caring people can we have a caring community. Its profound hope — based on the New Testament — springs from a recognition of human vulnerability to selfishness and our need to be changed. Having fewer illusions about the likely effects of political action, the church is a good agency for programmes of political education. Christians do not have to wait for the social revolution before they can find their experience transformed. The Kingdom of God is now.

Political questions are also moral and theological

Politics is not just about facts: it is also concerned with values. We cannot go far in this subject before we begin to raise moral and theological (or ideological) issues about the nature of man and his place in the universe. If we believe that man is no more than a clever animal, then we shall be moved to seek one kind of society, but if we believe that he is a moral and spiritual being, then our political strivings will take another direction. And it will not do to say that these matters do not concern us, that we are neutral about them. They force themselves on our attention and call for a decision. Positivism may be intellectually attractive, but it is not a practical possibility. Is the goal of all our striving to resemble an ant heap? Or are we looking for a free society with fellowship as a dominant theme? The intellectual discipline of sociology has developed in the last two centuries. It claims to be a science of men in society. Everything depends on what is meant by the claim. Sociology is a valuable, indispensable insight into the human condition, but it is a partial insight. It should not attempt to tell us everything, since it then strays beyond its brief and pretends to be a *philosophy, not a science*. This quickly becomes apparent in politics. Early on we encounter choices about values which are non-rational in the sense that they are not empirically demonstrable; they cannot be proved by logic alone, though this need not mean that they are irrational. Ethical and theological judgements are involved with politics from the beginning. They are not the only ingredients although we Christians have sometimes made the mistake of supposing they were. (In politics the struggle for power is prominent too.) But they cannot be ignored. It is time to give specific examples of this theme from the contemporary scene.

One way of expressing the Christian view of man is that we believe in human individualism and solidarity. First, we hold that every individual is a centre of value in himself, profoundly influenced of course by his environment and associations, but not entirely absorbed or explained by them. He has some freedom and choice, and is not merely a victim of his environment because he is not just a vegetable entirely produced by that environment. But secondly we believe that all these unique, disparate individuals belong to each other. Of course the groupings to which they belong are not unimportant — race, colour, creed, class. They help to give us our identity as British or Indian, young or old, rich or poor. But these groupings are not ultimately decisive, certainly not as important as our basic solidarity. The individualism and the solidarity of man — these two truths — we hold ultimately on the evidence of the crucified and risen Christ.

They will bring us into controversy with the two most prominent contenders for the political soul of British youth — the Communists and the National Front. "Individualism" conflicts with the first. Whether Karl Marx was strictly speaking an economic determinist is a matter of academic interest. But there can be no doubt that the movement which has sprung up in his name tends to see man primarily as a victim of an evil system, powerless to transform his experience until the day of the revolution. Christians may agree that the worker is alienated and exploited but not that he is, even in his present condition, entirely forsaken by his humanity or his God.

The activities of the National Front are, of course, divisive. Whatever their protestations, its members imply that colour creates an absolute difference. We do not dissent from the proposition that there are big cultural differences between various ethnic groups, but with the New Testament in hand, we deny that these differences are ultimate and unchangeable.

The churches as moral fellowships are among those national institutions which can attempt to handle the moral and ideological issues which are raised by politics. A Christian view of man and society is part of the raw material from which we may fashion our political philosophies and programmes. It would be a pity if the education of young people in the churches did not include the offer of this ingredient. The Christian religion is not an encyclopaedia of all knowledge and skills, but it does invite us to look at politics, as all else, in a different light.

Christians can argue without quarrelling

Recently I lived for a week in Belfast. And Protestant though I am, I stayed in the Falls Road area with a Catholic family. As the days passed, my admiration for my host increased. He was devoted to the cause of the unity of all Ireland and considered that the Roman Catholic community had suffered severe discrimination in Ulster. He intended to go on working for his beliefs — but non-violently. A gentle, strong creature, he would not tread on an insect or flinch before an emperor. He knew how to argue without quarrelling. This attitude was not unconnected with his personal faith. He was at once a highly sophisticated political animal and a convinced practising Christian. In a world where detente is a condition of survival, and men of very different persuasions must learn how to live together in unity and co-operation - Michael seemed to me a man of the future.

Ideally, Christians can argue without quarrelling. To make sense, that bald statement requires two comments. First, to say the least, Christians have not always lived up to this ideal. Secondly, Christians are not the only people who have the ability to argue without quarrelling. All that is claimed here is that such tolerance belongs to the nature of their faith.

If this is true, then it should answer the objections of those Christians who think that the introduction of politics will bring controversy into the life of the church and destroy the spirit of good fellowship. It is not by pretending that we have no differences and conflicts, that Christians will grow closer to each other; rather, fellowship grows among those believers who acknowledge, accept and tolerate their differences, because though these differences are seen to be real, they are not experienced as absolute. Clean controversy is quite consistent with concepts of Christian conduct!

It is often assumed today that Christians are people who will not take sides on controversial issues and do not have strong opinions. They are expected to be among the vast army of "don't knows" on the major social and political subjects of our time. If that were true, they would be anaemic nonentities. The present view is that they should have commitments and loyalties. They ought to care about what happens to their own people whether on the basis of class or nation; so, for example, they can be patriots and also fighters for working-class rights.

But along with other groups, they hold their political views with several qualifications:

(i) They are not dogmatically closing their minds to opposing points of view. They do not suppose that to them and them alone has been revealed the final, absolute and complete political truth. They can see some truth in their opponent's position; it is only that the balance of the argument seems to lie on the stand they have taken. But this should not inhibit them from the most vigorous pursuit of their aims and objectives.

(ii) They do not judge all who disagree with them must be either fools or knaves. They do not put dunce's caps or horns on the heads of their political opponents. They do not allow their political judgements, however strongly held, to affect their personal relationships.

(iii) They recognize that their political choices are influenced, albeit unconsciously, by their own self-interest. In Christian language, they acknowledge that sin has affected their political choices and they need to repent. This means that they will never see their commitment as wholly God-given and their opponents as moved by the devil. Further, it means that in any political conflict, they will admit that there is some wrong on their side — before the judgement of God — as well as on the side of their enemies. The adoption of this attitude would in many places take the heat out of political conflicts where Christians are involved, all around the world. Reconciliation is impossible when both sides believe they have all the righteousness and refuse to repent. "True democracy begins with confession of our sins" (W. H. Auden).

Of course, it does not always happen like this. Sadly one must admit that there are places — like Cyprus and Northern Ireland — where religion reinforces community prejudice and conflict: where the battle rages more fiercely because each warring community has convinced itself that "God is on our side", that it is only their enemies who have to open their eyes to the truth and repent. When this happens to Christian groups — as sometimes in Northern Ireland — then the churches have become the captives of a particular political ideology and God is being used to serve a political end. That is a result of one kind of Christian involvement with the world which most Christians outside the situation would not want to see. More important is the claim that it does not reflect the intention of the gospel or the general message of the New Testament. Neither of these allows us to give absolute value to our political judgements. And to all who

act as though they do, one wishes to repeat the message of
Cromwell to the General Assembly of the Church of Scotland
on the 3rd August 1650: "I beseech you in the bowels of Christ,
think it possible you may be mistaken."

These realities, however, do not detract from the general
position among Christian congregations, perhaps in less stress-
ful areas. Here it is more likely that political judgements are not
seen as absolute and are submitted to the judgement of God.

If all this is true, then it follows that the church is a good
situation in which to have programmes of political education.
For what is most unattractive about many political advocates is
their ugly dogmatism, their refusal to admit uncertainty, their
reluctance to submit their beliefs to critical examination. We
notice this on the extremes both of the Left and the Right, but it
is the former who are usually more articulate about their views
and have written more books about them. Sometimes they
regard their conclusions as infallible and revealed truth. Anybody therefore who dares to question them is either wilfully
blind or stupid.

They see the whole world as lying under the power of the evil
one — only it is not the devil as in the Scriptures, but the
capitalist system which exploits the workers and divides the
population into the haves and have-nots. The best-known
advocate of this point of view is Alinskey. "Liberals charge
radicals with passionate partisanship. To this accusation the
radical's jaw tightens as he snaps 'Guilty' — we are partisan for
the people. Furthermore, we know that all people are partisan.
The only non-partisan people are those who are dead. You too
are partisan — if not for the people, then for whom?"[2] According to this view, it is only by direct action — rent strikes,
obstructing main roads, squatting, boycotts, that change is to
be effected, and no improvement can be achieved by infiltrating
into positions of power. Moreover, the basic interpretation is
not to be questioned and anybody who does raise any objection
is to be regarded as having a personal interest in doing so.

It is a movement with a big emotional appeal especially for
the oppressed and those who sympathize with the oppressed.
Whether it is likely to lead to sustained progress is another question. Another issue is raised. When any political group says that
its truth is self-evident, beyond the reach of scrutiny, then is
there any hope for co-operation? What are we to say to the

P.L.O., the Moluccan terrorists in Holland, and the Klu Klux Klan who also maintain that their truths are self-evident and beyond the reach of scrutiny?

Christians disagree with the extremists who have no doubts. Education cannot take place in a setting where the conclusions are known beforehand. We do not deny that societies are places of conflict or that there is painful exploitation and deprivation: we also want to fight so that human beings may fulfil their possibilities. But we do not think that conflict and poverty are the only features of the human situation. And we do not conclude that those who will not forget everything else are faithless. A church is a good agency for political education precisely because it will not want to impose one political dogma on everybody, since in the judgement of God all our political judgements are imperfect.

Suggested guidelines for the involvement of Christians in politics

This last section brings together some of the main points made in chapters one and three and summarizes the argument so far.

1. The active involvement of Christians in politics is a matter of theology: in other words, it rests on what they believe God to be like as he has revealed himself in the Bible and supremely in Jesus Christ. Therefore it should never be an attempt to up-date the church or to win support. The God of the Bible is involved in the affairs of men, opposing injustice of all kinds and working for social righteousness as well as individual goodness. His followers will join in the same struggle or they may find he is no longer in their midst. Amos pronounced the judgement of God upon his churchgoing contemporaries because they sold the poor for silver and the needy for a pair of shoes.[3] Not all religion is good: its practice can be immoral and degrading. Christians should be involved in politics not because they believe in God but because they believe in the God of the Bible. Moreover, the biblical "myth"[4] of the Fall implies that sin is located not only in the bad choices made by individuals or in their disposition to behaviour that falls short of the mark. Sin is a cosmic reality, part of our dreadful legacy, and it has worked its demonic way into the systems under which we live — social, economic, political, and international. The biblical theme is not

so much that there are good and bad people, but that all are living in a fallen world. "If you then being evil . . ." says Jesus (Matthew 7:11). Paul is quite explicit not only that our best individual deeds are tainted with some egotism, and self-seeking through anxiety and insecurity, but that evil is expressed corporately. For him evil is more than the bad deeds of individual men and women: it is cosmic and indeed supra-mundane. "For our fight is not against human foes, but against cosmic powers, against the authorities and potentates of this dark world, against the superhuman forces of evil in the heavens" (Ephesians 6:12, NEB). Paul is equally sure that the salvation Christ brings is cosmic as well as individual. "Yet always there was hope, because the universe itself is to be freed from the shackles of mortality and enter upon the liberty and the splendour of the children of God. Up to the present, we know, the whole created universe groans in all its parts as if in the pangs of child birth" (Romans, 7:21, 22, NEB). If all this is true, then it follows that Christians cannot content themselves with an evangelism which aims only at the conversion of individuals. They must look and work for redemption in the whole of the world's life including its economic, social, political and international systems.

2. Though the Bible gives no precise instructions for the decisions of Christians in political situations, yet clear principles are offered. The Bible leave us in no doubt about the kind of society of which God would approve.

Donald Hay[5] has provided a valuable account of biblical teaching about economics. Man is to use the material resources of the earth but as God's steward. Man has the right to have work which is meaningful, purposeful and contributes to his sense of community. On the distribution of income, Hay argues that the Bible shows God's will to be that everybody should share in the earthly bounty but nobody should want or use too much.

With these principles in mind, Hay has no difficulty in showing that capitalism is defective and sinful in some of its aspects. It offends against all three canons. Some will take this verdict to mean a revival of the common fear that Christian involvement in politics implies an inevitable left-wing bias. The case is slightly different. The Bible describes the ideal intentions of God and therefore any political and economic system which man creates will come under the judgement of God. Christians will find themselves critical of aspects of any society where they live, be it capitalist or socialist. A Church which has no quarrel with the world has no message for the world. Ours is still a capitalist society where the private sector accounts for at least 75% of total employment. It is inevitable therefore than when from the distinctive perspective of the Bible, contemporary Christians criticise features of their society, they direct their attention against capitalism. With Bible in hand, the Christian is never satisfied. In a revealing passage, Lesslie Newbigin describes his feelings when he passes from West Berlin to East Berlin — "when I contrast the grim totalitarianism on the one side with the screaming futilitarianism on the other".[6]

3. But God's ideal intentions are not immediately realizable on earth. Attempts to make them so are sometimes counterproductive. We cannot legislate for saints. Christians have to learn to be idealists without illusions — to listen for God's word in ugly contemporary reality. They have to "compromise" — there is no avoiding the unacceptable word. Again and again they are confronted by situations where God's perfect will is not immediately apparent and they must seek the greater of two "goods" and the lesser of two evils. Jesus recognized this sombre fact when he said that though a life-long union of husband and wife was God's intention, yet divorce was permitted by Moses on account of the hardness of men's hearts. (Matthew 19: 3-9). "We must look for a second best in a sinful world . . . So our approach to whatever economic systems we live under will be realistic and pragmatic, not losing sight of the ideal, but acknowledging that the ideal is unattainable in political terms" (Hay). Hence of course arise the many political differences among Christians, sometimes proving divisive and destructive. But these differences come from the "givenness" of the situation. At least if we start from the Bible we shall gain two advantages. First — whatever our compromises, we shall never completely lose sight of the ideal. Second — we shall not claim that our own commitment to a particular political policy or programme is God's will for everybody.

4. Churches — both national and local — will be chary of committing themselves to one political philosophy or programme. All suggestions that every Christian should belong to one party are ludicrous. They are also unfair since the Church

should welcome into its fold people of every political persuasion. Of course, there are some issues where a proposed course
of action is clean contrary to the gospel and it is right that a call
should go out for the whole church to be united in opposition.
Measures aimed at the promotion of racism, the denial of
human rights, or restriction of religious freedom — all these are
examples. But many political issues are not about ends — on
which all men of goodwill are agreed — but about the best
means to achieve those ends. The widespread unemployment of
school-leavers is a calamity to be avoided. But whether this is
better achieved by more state ownership of the means of
production and distribution, or by the encouragement of
private enterprise — that is a matter on which different Christians will hold contrasting views. And they ought not to learn
that their church has committed them as a matter of faith, to a
point of view with which they are not in sympathy. Admittedly,
it is not always easy to draw the line between issues which are
respectively concerned with "ends" and "means".

5. However, for the individual Christian, the matter is very
different. More of us should be involved in political movements
which in our view offer the best hope of moving our society
closer to God's intention. We are not just to have political
thoughts, but to act politically, committing ourselves resolutely
to what we have understood of God's will, seeking forgiveness
throughout for our imperfect apprehension. Repentance for the
inadequacy of his views and the recognition that his own
interests affect his decision, will be a distinctive mark of the
Christian in politics. But repentance will not inhibit action. It is
part of the recognition that the mission of the Church to the
world is shared by the whole people of God, called not to read
"segregation" for "congregation", invited to go into human
situations where God is not acknowledged, not to preach, but to
hear the Word of God in an unexpected place. So we might
begin to look for a new style of discipleship, particularly among
young Christians. They should more frequently join with
pressure groups like Shelter and Child Care; organize to fight
against the exploitation of man by man and nature by all of us;
help God, by political means, to change an unjust and
threatened world. The chronic weakness of Christians is to have
"right thoughts without action", to suppose that discipleship
consists of possessing a theology. Many young Christians today

insist that we should act upon our beliefs in resisting injustice in society and in this struggle discover what are the right beliefs.

6. Christians will not hope for too much from political action. They will not suppose that the fashionable word, "emancipation", completely covers the meaning of an older word, "redemption". It is scepticism not cynicism which will lead them to ask how far a moral society can make moral men. Governments have a moral function, but it is limited; they can do much to encourage the welfare and fulfilment of individual citizens, but not everything. One of the demonic pretensions of our time is that there are purely political answers to human dilemmas. Individual responsibility and local initiative are also essential ingredients of human welfare. The state can for example do much, be legislation and benefits, to encourage a sound stable family life, but the happiness and fulfilment found in a single family depends even more on many individual choices and attitudes within that family. Christians on the political scene never forget that people are not vegetables at the mercy of their environment. They do not remind us so often that we are victims that we are unlikely ever to be victors. On the contrary, they assure us that we can enter the kingdom of God now, without waiting for the social revolution: that only Christ and ourselves can provide the true freedom. We may find that some of the assumptions of our colleagues in programmes of political education cut across this Christian view of man and society.

If Christians need political education, it is no less true that enthusiasts for political education often need Christians, to save them from present utopianism and future despair. We can go even further, though, as experience demonstrates, we shall have to be tactful about it. At the right moment, and depending upon a relationship already established, we may share our conviction that the best hopes of "secular" man are feasible only on the basis of a Christian view of the world.

7. In working with other organizations for a better society, the church must be an example even before it is an oracle. Ideally, the church is a foretaste of the Kingdom, an anticipation of what God intends the whole world to be. Sadly, we are not like that, but there can be some evidence that we have not entirely forgotten our destiny. It is easy to catalogue the worst obscenities in this tragic world. The greed of some leads to the impoverishment of many — 650 million people on the earth are

trying to live on 10p a day each. In the northern hemisphere, we are using up the earth's irreplaceable resources to maintain an unnatural and wasteful standard of living. Even in developed countries citizens are often treated impersonally by huge bureaucratic institutions. Possessions and money are the touchstone of success and a man's social prestige is measured by his job. The catalogue of woe is endless. But the question now is whether things are the same in the church. Or is it a city set on a hill in a dark and "naughty world"? Being a society that demonstrably does not conform to the world's materialistic standards will be more effective than issuing statements on political issues. To a degree, this does happen now though it appears mainly in a sensitivity to personal relationships unmatched by an appreciation of how social, political and economic structures affect the experience of the individual. In many respects, the church is still the most loving large institution in our society. And sometimes, whilst not engaging in direct political activity, it behaves in a way that will make possible future political change. Early in the last century, the minister of the Coke Memorial Church, Kingston, Jamaica, broke the law by welcoming black slaves to services in daylight hours. For repeated transgression his church was closed for seven years. He did not directly agitate against slavery, but who can doubt that when emancipation finally came, his gesture had played a small part?

All this — and much else in like vein — is true, but as they move into an era of deeper political involvement, Christians should constantly remind themselves that to be an example is at once more costly and effective than to be an oracle. A politically-conscious church will still devote much of its energy to acts of personal service. This is because it refuses to put all its eggs in the basket of a revolution. There may be no remedy for people's distress apart from a new system, but that need not mean that nothing can be done to help hard-pressed people before the revolution. The world may be evil but the Christian constantly discerns possibilities of good through compassion.

Whilst we wait for the revolution, much can be done to humanize the worst effects of an unjust system. But a politically-conscious church, whilst engaging in these frequent acts of compassion, and attempts at humanization, will recognize that there is a political dimension to the problems of those whom they serve.

8. Despite what has been said about the hope that in the future more churches will join political movements, it has to be recognized that the major contribution to political change by the church, will be in the direction of changing public attitudes. This is not to be understood as the encouragement of a passive acceptance of injustices and deprivation. But the reality is that we cannot have a caring community unless we have a lot of caring people. Policies of justice can grow only in a climate of public opinion where we are concerned about our neighbour as well as ourselves and our own group interests. Few problems in Britain could not be solved if most of us were prepared to live more simply and less wastefully and supported policies which expressed this detachment. Since many of our problems lie in public attitudes, it is to a change in public attitudes that we must look for the long term solvent. I know many Christians in Northern Ireland who are working with small groups at grass-roots level to create reconciliation and understanding between the two sides. They have no immediate solution to complex political dilemmas but who can deny that they are helping to create a human situation in which some political solution can be found? How noble are the hopes expressed by some of the writers on political education! Yet one cannot always throw off the misgiving that much of it is based on an unrealistic view of the human situation. Our Christian forbears were not wrong in thinking that they had to concentrate their efforts on pastoral care for the individual and inter-personal relations. They were wrong, as we can see with the benefit of hindsight, only when they supposed that individual goodness would be enough without political organizations.

9. Nor should we forget another specialized rôle which the church — along with other movements — can play in this matter of political activity. This is to keep up the morale of the participants, to foster their belief that the struggle is worthwhile and not without meaning and hope. And we are able to do this sometimes even for those who cannot share to the full the Christian faith.

In any context, morale is vital; it helps us to achieve what represents more than the sum total of our abilities; it fosters self-confidence. That is one of the reasons why football teams usually play better in home fixtures. The support of the home crowd lifts their morale and raises their game. When W. F. Whyte[6] investigated the patterns of leadership in a gang of young men in New York, he found that their successes at bowling were directly related not only to their skill, but to their popularity rating with the members and the amount of support they received from the spectators when they played.

In a different setting, morale is important for continued political struggle. Though our colleagues may not be able or willing to articulate it in these terms, they often need an underlying conviction that life has a meaning and a purpose. The threat to the secularist in political activity is that he will be driven to one of two sad conclusions — either that history has no goal and one must concentrate on an unquestioning individualism — or that in the vast processes of history, the individual has no significance. Without complacency, one hopes, it may be said that it is this dilemma which has been solved for the Christian by the work of God in Christ, who acts in history and is bringing history to an ultimate climax, yet has a purpose which can find a place for the single life. Without some such conviction, however deeply buried, the political activist may lose his nerve, which is the vulnerability of the secular humanist; or he may lose his enthusiasm and (as somebody wrote of Napoleon) remember the words of the revolution but forget the tunes. Sometimes, the Christian going out into the world, with much to learn from "secular" situations, finds himself engaged in an unexpected ministry, trying to keep alive the best hopes of his secular colleagues.

10. If — in the careful sense in which it has been defined — Christians are to move more actively into the field of political action, then they will have to display a willingness to accept that we live in a world where interests and ideas are in conflict. And that these conflicts will be reflected in the church and should be brought into open scrutiny. At present we too often operate on the principle that good fellowship must exclude honest differences. Conflict is one of the most important things that ever happens to a group. Most of the gold to be mined is there. Working through conflicts of interests and ideas may lead, not to estrangement, but to deeper understanding, to positive action, and to the growth and development of the group and individuals. We shall not advance into the political field (where a battle is constantly being fought over the allocation of scarce

resources) if we work with a model of a church where only "nice things" are said rather than a place where we accept each other and our differences because we all have something greater in common. It is doubly strange that we should fail here. For we share with Communists (exploitation of the worker) an insight (original sin) that something has gone quite seriously wrong with this world. In addition we learn from the Bible that one effect of the Word of God is to make men argue with one another — and with God.

In colleagueship with Marxists, I have found them sometimes so dominated by the notion of conflict, that they seem to be unable to see anything else. But equally I have found many Christians unwilling to accept and admit that there is any conflict of competing economic interests in their society. Mentally, they enclose their community in a sentimental cocoon. One of the urgent educational tasks of the church today is to help us all to understand two realities. (1) What Christians can learn from Marxism; what true insights it offers for our understanding of the human situation; where it contains the judgement of God. (2) What in Marxism is unacceptable to Christians. The issue is complicated because the original Marxist doctrines have not remained unchanged with the passage of time, or gone unchallenged by those who would today call themselves Marxists.[7]

Along with Darwin, Einstein and Freud, Marx has compelled us to think of the world and the human situation in fresh ways. The influence of these thinkers has not been confined to students of their original works. Their ideas have become common currency, part of the subconscious assumptions of our daily lives. Christian education programmes cannot pretend they have never been or thought. The church may not exist in an intellectual ghetto. We have to take account of their abiding insight and ask whether we can still hold to a distinctive insight of the Christian faith. This process can prove valuable since it helps us to come to terms with hidden attitudes and assumptions within ourselves, which, if unacknowledged, are a hindrance both to personal development and political education.

If more Christians move into the fields of political action, they will find themselves working with some colleagues who speak a new language. They use the words of revolution, and sometimes of violent revolution. They believe that improvement can come only by smashing the present system and replacing it by collective ownership of the means of production and distribution. The Christian has to decide how far he can share this outlook, guided as he is by a biblical view of life and by the facts of the situation confronting him. He will of course be deeply disturbed by some of the things he finds in his society and want to work with others for change. He will argue that following Christ today includes action on the political front. No less than Marx, he may think that the time has come not to understand the world but to change it. His radicalism may be no less extreme than that of the Marxist, but he will not suggest that this approach is required from all Christians. He will have serious misgivings about the use of force in gaining improvement and will want to ask many questions about its humanization. And though he knows that political action is required, he will have no illusions that of itself this can lead to human fulfilment. At present,the pity is that many in the churches suppose that involvement in politics inevitably means an association with godless Marxism.

4
The present position in the churches

Political attitudes in the churches today vary widely reflecting the differences in the secular world. Moreover the churches relate to the political powers in various ways.

(i) As an organized body, the church has to negotiate with the state to secure the best means of ensuring its survival and effective operation as a worshipping and witnessing body. In some countries, it is recognized that the state has some part to play in the life of the church. In Sweden it has intervened in the matter of women clergy. In Britain, bishops are officially appointed by the Queen and a few decades ago, the reform of the Prayer Book was a matter of parliamentary debate. Elsewhere, the church may have to look for political means to defend itself against an unsympathetic state. When I worshipped with the Baptists in Moscow and Kiev, I found the people singing hymns from words copied in exercise books because the Soviet government would not permit the printing of more hymn books. For the same reason, many of the worshippers begged me to send them a Bible. Political action by the churches had failed to gain permission for a further supply.

(ii) Elsewhere, there is another political alignment of the churches. It consists of their association with the conservative forces of reaction against any threat of revolution and change, a pattern of alignment which links the church with the established powers as representing stability, tradition and authority. Despite repression and injustice in South Korea, the state was identified as "Christian" fighting against the atheistic North in the 1950s. We sometimes have the mortification of hearing on the news that "the Christians have opened a new offensive in Beirut". The largest Christian denomination in South Africa supports a policy of racial discrimination as part of its political duty.

(iii) By contrast, there are groups of Christians — notably in the South American continent — who see it as their Christian duty to oppose the existing political system of oppression and injustice, in some cases even to the point of taking up arms against it. "A revolutionary process is shaking the Church out of its routine and presenting it with various options. The Church must become an 'agent of action' within the process, or it will inevitably be reactionary against it."[1] "There is no Latin American country where this phenomenon, which shocks many people and gives hope to many others — the commitment of the Christians and the Church to revolution — has failed to express itself. It has become somewhat a matter of routine to see repression, jail, exile, torture and also death reaching Catholic priests and nuns."[2] Painful as it can be for Christians in those countries, they have one consolation. The issues are clear: the religious task and the political task are the same. Liberation in Christ includes liberation from the oppressor. In countries where the state has been more deeply influenced by Christian ideas of compassion and justice, the choices for believers are not always so clear-cut. The form and content of our religion owes much to our social circumstances and those who are in positions of severe disadvantage will more readily understand that the gospel promises liberation from the oppressor.

(iv) There is a feature of church involvement in economic, social and political matters which has become prominent in the post-war period. The churches through commissions, councils and much literature have shown themselves aware that they should be concerned with everything that affects the life of people; that they should confront all those depersonalizing and destructive forces which darken the modern scene; that they should be the enemies of poverty, tyranny, homelessness, war, racial discrimination and the rest. The enemy is any system which defaces the divine image in man. It would be difficult for one mind to encompass all the material that has been issued under this heading in the last twenty years, all of it projecting the churches as the champions of human rights.[3] But perhaps the new outlook was neatly summarized by Pope John when he said that the gospel is "for all men and for the whole man". The movement represents a tardy recognition that personality is largely a social product and that social conditions are a decisive factor in human fulfilment, though it leads inevitably to controversy among Christians: but the present view is that this can be valuable. In recent years, few political events have stirred so much debate in the churches as the grant from the World Council of Churches to the Patriotic Front in Rhodesia. Should this be regretted? It illustrates the agonizing choices Christians have to make. Moreover, it is encouraging to find Christians debating such an issue among themselves.

Nor should we omit to mention another kind of political involvement of Christians, significant enough even though it engages only a tiny minority of believers. This is the search for "an alternative society" by the setting up of Christian "communes" where a group of people live under another "political system". Perhaps the project at Taizé in France is the best-known of these experiments and it has attracted world-wide attention.[4] At its best, the whole enterprise of "communes" expresses more than a despair of the world in its present form or a retreat. It even goes beyond the best reason for mediaeval monasticism, namely that the world is in such a mess that the only rational course is to withdraw and pray for it. Ideally "Christian communes" aim to provide archetypes of a new kind of human association. They represent an attempt of Christians to be an example rather than an oracle. As such they may exert a big influence. They can be cities set on hills, a constant and healthy rebuke to the rest of us who in another sense "remain in the world". But they are unlikely to attract a large following and they are unlikely to be decisive in efforts to make political education part of the normal diet of church life.

Among Christian groups in England the range of attitudes to the political scene could be plotted on a continuum of deepening interest in political activities:

(i) It is evil, keep away from it. "Politics" represents part of the devil's domain. Curiously, this is not unlike the Marxist conviction that political parties will disappear after the Revolution.

(ii) It is irrelevant for the Christian, since he has a hope that makes politics fade into insignificance.

(iii) Christians must act politically to preserve their freedom of worship.

(iv) The reform of individuals will lead to a new political system and therefore concentration on evangelism is supremely relevant politically. This may be linked with the conviction that "politics" is seeking a secular solution for problems that are moral and spiritual.

(v) Christians must show an awareness of the plight óf the poor and the oppressed and help individuals wherever they can. This may be associated with a feeling that "politics" means "party politics" — divisive, partisan, a struggle for power. (My enquiries have revealed that many of the different attitudes of Christian groups on this matter are rooted in the different meanings that they give to the word "politics".) But Christians must be good citizens.

(vi) Christians should learn about the realities of the "secular" situation, for example, about how poor agricultural methods contribute to hunger. (But with no recognition tht evil may have worked itself into the economic systems of the world.)

(vii) Christians recognize that part of our troubles may be due to an immoral system as well as immoral men and women and that improvements depend partly on political action.

(viii) Christians join with others outside the church in political movements, in pressure groups who organize and act to effect change in the law and in the economic and social system. This is seen as God's fight too.

(ix) Christians, despairing of improvements by constitutional means, join movements of direct political action.

The developments described earlier are trying to move Christians to that part of the spectrum which recognizes the necessity of political action. It might be thought that this state of affairs should greatly encourage the advocates of the point of view represented in these pages. For clarity's sake let us briefly re-state this perspective. God as revealed in the Bible has many attributes. One of them is that he is the God of history, working to create his kingdom of compassion and justice. He is engaged in many activities. One of them is to be present on the contemporary scene, protecting the poor, the deprived and the oppressed. And a part — though not the whole — of the believer's obedience is to ask how he can be God's fellow-worker in this endeavour. So the harsh and ugly realities of the modern situation are the raw material of his discipleship as well as, and as part of, his vision of the eternal God.

May it not be said that some of the developments described above contribute to this definition? They do, but in practice and whatever the original intention, they suffer from one fatal defect, previously described. They are politics without political education. They result in a situation where our leaders are very active politically on our behalf but they do not engage the whole people of God in the struggle for freedom and justice: their weighty pronouncements by-pass most congregations. They produce a few star performers but not a church which is politically educated and active. Anyone who doubts the truth of this statement and thinks perhaps that it is a harsh judgement should do what I have done over the past decade — visit many churches in different parts of the country and ask what version of the gospel is being presented in worship, service and action. (The great exceptions are the "ethnic" churches, mostly West Indian, which exhibit a high degree of political awareness chiefly because two concerns of their membership are achieving social identity for themselves and gaining justice for their group). The local church is still often the most living institution in a neighbourhood — and long may it remain so. But usually there is no answering echo to the church leaders' cry for Christians to engage in the struggle for human rights. Judged by the content of many sermons, it seems that a whole dimension of the biblical God has been lost in the local church. He is the God of the individual soul, consoling us in our sorrows, reinforcing our own most encouraging self-image, strengthening family life. He has become the doctor of the soul rather than the God of history. The theology of the local church fashions many of its activities, most of which are excellent and should not be forgotten. They provide a valuable supportive service for hard-pressed and lonely people. In a society of large bureaucratic institutions, the church is often one of the few smaller associations — outside the family — where we can be known as unique individuals, where we have a name and do not have to be given a number. The local church is often a network of personal relationships. It plays an important part in the religious education of the young and this function may expand with the questions hanging over compulsory religious teaching in state schools. The local church can bring radiance and fulfilment to those who belong. But with all this, there is one thing missing. The local church does not usually mobilize people to fight injustice in the local or wider community. Its main efforts are directed towards persuading people to have mystical experiences, to support the church as an organization, to preserve a Christian view of life that is more and more unfashionable and to accept the counsel of the church in coping with their emotional problems. So whatever its overt aims, local Christian leadership tends to reproduce followers in its own bourgeois image. The moral and spiritual power generated in local churches is usually in neutral gear as far as the social problems of the neighbourhood are concerned.

In the worst cases "congregation" means "segregation". Believers are withdrawn from the world to worship for a time; they are not enrolled for mission, or sent out to listen for God's word in situations where he is not known and acknowledged.

When they contemplate public issues, local churches are marked by two features. First, they experience a gravitational pull towards "law and order". Second, they over-stress a valuable point, that there can be no enduring social righteousness that is not supported by much individual goodness. They neglect the converse truth that evil in the system will encourage evil in the individual. Ideally, a local church should demonstrate constantly the inter-play of individual goodness and social righteousness. And though they may not of themselves be able to change social and political systems, they should at least appreciate the social and political dimensions of the problems of those they seek to help.

Recently in a local church council, the leaders faced the question, "What can we do to involve the young people in the work of the church?" After due consideration, only one positive suggestion emerged. "Invite some of them to help to take up the collection at the services." Presumably if they performed efficiently in this area they might graduate to cutting the sandwiches on social occasions! The lack of suggestions was symptomatic of a church which is introverted. As a matter of fact, much excellent work is done in that church, but it is almost entirely devoted to strengthening the organization and helping individuals in their personal lives. Much social work of a personal service nature is undertaken. But the notion that the church and each of its members has a mission in the world is overlooked. True, they collect large sums of money to help the missionaries and for aid to poor countries, but for people whom they are unlikely to see and whose social, economic and political circumstances they are not taught to comprehend.

Some will argue that it is enough that our leaders — usually full-time professionals — should act politically on our behalf. They have the time and the competence to deal with these highly technical matters. The political witness of the church needs to be organized to bring the maximum influence to bear in the places where decisions are made. None of these factors should be despised. But by themselves they overlook one reality which if we are right, is central to the meaning of the Christian movement. It is that the mission of God is to be undertaken by the people of God, though this principle leaves room to recognize diversities of gifts. To each and every believer Jesus Christ has said both, "Come — to me" and "Go — to the world". That is why, it seems to me, we cannot limit ourselves to "politics without political education".

The point has been well put in a much-neglected pamphlet by Professor Walter James.[5] Writing as a Christian believer, he deplores the fact that voluntary organizations, such as the church, are prone to concern themselves solely with individual piety and make acts of charity their response to social problems and issues. But when voluntary organizations begin to work for social change, there arises the further question of power. How do they wish to effect change? Is it only by the activities of the gifted few who impose their solutions on the many? Or is it to be by attempts to involve the whole constituency in the process of beneficient change?

"At one extreme there are those who wish little or no change to occur. These I will call the Preservers. At the other extreme there are those whom I will call the Transformers. The second attitude is that which is concerned with the distribution of power: that is the capacity to prevent changes or to choose which changes to make. At one extreme there are those who think affairs are managed best when they are left to the qualified: whether qualified by birth, wealth or professional training. This position I will call Aristocratic — those who inhabit it are literally supporters of rule by the best people. At the other extreme from them are those who would see power best exercised when decisions are made by all who are affected by them. This position I will call Democratic."[6]

With this analysis, Walter James constructs a typology of those engaged in society's affairs. The *Aristocratic Preservers* wish to use the powers of those best qualified to lead to resist change. The *Aristocratic Transformers* wish to see change controlled by the élitist minority who are qualified to decide those matters. The *Democratic Preservers* look for a popular movement to retain traditional beliefs and practices. The *Democratic Transformers* want to see change achieved by the spread of the decision-making powers.

It is the present contention that the last type represents, on the contemporary scene, the closest approximation to the servants of the Kingdom of God and that of the four, it derives most logically from the fact of Christ, crucified and risen. If God's intention is to re-make his children in the likeness of Christ — who is, in Luther's phrase, "the proper man" — then it is the Democratic Preservers who should be encouraged in the churches. This is not to deny that their path is the most diifficult to tread.

With this in mind, we turn to consider the youth policies and programmes of the churches. They still have a major stake in the educational enterprise of Britain. If we confine our attention only to the over-twelves, there are probably several million young people who meet on church premises every week. The organizations[7] to which they belong have differing forms of affiliation with the organized churches. Some, like the Methodist Association of Youth Clubs, are sponsored and organized by a denomination and they are concerned to promote the ethos of their organization, though it by no means follows that only those who belong to the denomination can be members of the movement. Other movements — like the Boys' Brigade — are not linked in the same way to one denomination, though their stated aims are specifically Christian, and each local group is associated with a local church. In many cases, the ties of Scouts and Guides with local churches are more tenuous; in fact, the group may be "sponsored" or "open". The picture is not complete unless we include "para-church" organizations, movements which are interdenominational and which usually exist to stress a particular aspect of Christian discipleship or to identify a particular approach. They include Frontier Youth Trust,

Scripture Union and Corrymeela. As we shall see, they are in a position to make a special contribution in this matter of political education.

Nearly all these movements are organized nationally and through democratically-elected representatives and committees, and full-time staff, they work out policies and programmes, offer guidance, support and service to local units. All the major churches in fact have their own "youth" or "education" departments. All of them, of course, are aware of the general pressures and arguments in Britain for the political education of the young which have been described in Chapter Two. And they have to make a response to these developments unless they want to announce to the world that they are still living in the past. In 1978, for example, the traditional youth movements had to decide whether they would send delegates to the Youth Festival in Cuba. How have these organisations, at varying levels of church affiliation, responded to the challenge in policy-statements and plans? There are four main categories.

Primarily Evangelistic

Faced by mounting pressures, some have insisted that their main — in some cases even their sole — objective is the conversion of the individual to the Christian faith leading to membership of the Church. This is the "pearl of great price" and these people are not to be distracted by lesser pearls!

"We have at no time sought to include political education in any of our programmes. Our aim is to present the claims of Jesus Christ", wrote one organization in reply to my enquiry. Another movement recognizes that some of their members would regard political involvement as sinful, though it is significant that this occurs when "political parties" are thought of. "Some feel that a Christian should play a fuller part and be involved in political parties and political work, whilst others feel that as citizens of heaven the Christian should not be so involved. Others feel that Christians should not even vote."

But in general, the outlook is not so narrow. Alongside this exclusively evangelistic emphasis are commonly found four, more liberal aspects. It is expected that conversion will lead to good citizenship. "The ultimate aim of our work is to bring young people to a Christian way of life involving personal commitment: this in turn leads to a concern to be good citizens among the society in which they grow up which hopefully will include a constructive interest in politics" (Crusaders). Moreover, those movements inspire programmes of personal service for others. Thus, one of the aims of The Christian Alliance is "to carry out other charitable purposes for the advancement of their intellectual, social and physical welfare . . ." For the young people themselves, they offer programmes of activities that are more than narrowly religious exercises, and cater for mind, body and spirit. Finally, some of these movements recognize that they supplement the work of the local church where more general teaching may be offered. But with all this there is a massive concentration on personal evangelism.

It is of course a tenable and perfectly respectable position. At least the advocates are taking a clear stand. We know where we are with them. They do not overtly go along with the current fashion whilst covertly practising an approach of individual piety. And all of them would claim that when individuals have personal faith in Christ they become better citizens and make a larger contribution to the social good.

Thus, the perspective is not without its merits; to a degree, it would be shared by most people who engage in youth work with a Christian motivation. But from the present standpoint it has defects. It overlooks that this attempt to be politically neutral, ultimately gives tacit support to the present system of society. So the "Evangelicals" are likely to encourage the "Preservers" rather than the "Transformers". Oddly enough — and we shall return to this point — the "Evangelicals" who firmly believe in the reality of sin, have not always understood that sin has worked itself into the social, economic and political systems in which we live and that their converts must live out their lives of devotion in a world where politics will affect their daily experience. Are we offering them an adequate preparation unless we help them to comprehend that reality?

But there is a deeper and even more paradoxical issue to be discussed with the "Evangelicals". They would be happy with the title "Bible Christians" and they regard the Scriptures as the ultimate authority for their outlook and activities. But we are compelled to ask them whether their attitude reflects the God of the Bible or only one part of his nature. This is not just a clever dialectical device to hoist them with their own petard. It is part of the agonising search for reality in which Christians are often engaged today. Is the God of the Bible concerned only with the individual soul, energetic in snatching "brands from the burning"? Or is he also depicted there as the God of the nations, working for social righteousness as well as individual holiness? There is a proper division of labour among Christian educators. It is arguable that one proper specialism is concentration on the conversion of individuals and the nourishment of their inner life. But do the "Evangelicals" always recognize the place of other Christian partners whose special responsibility is to help young Christians to question the present system, to "come of age" in Christ and among men, and to worship the God of history?

Social Educators

Christians in this category are operating on a broader front. They want to help young people to grow and develop in all aspects of their experience, to live in this world as well as to prepare themselves for that which is to come. They know that Youth Service changes its character as it seeks to respond to contemporary needs. They realize that it is no longer primarily concerned with providing basic education as it was for Hannah More and Elizabeth Fry at the end of the eighteenth century; or meeting basic economic needs as it was for Neumann, a pioneer in Boys' Club work in the nineteenth century. Youth work is always a "gap-filler"; it aims to provide for a large number of youngsters what they really need but do not find in the institutionalized provision. And when we ask what is left out today for many young people in Britain, the broad answer is "social education". This includes the skill and confidence to develop and sustain a range of different personal relationships, the confidence to develop talents, and to make a happy, fulfilling and, generally socially-acceptable use of leisure. "Social education" also includes learning how to take your place in the larger community as spouse, parent and citizen. One of the few universal aims of voluntary youth work through its 200 years' history is "preparation for citizenship". This is where the aim impinges on political education and we can find many examples of it in the literature of the social educators.

Typical of this approach is the Christian Endeavour Union: "We seek to confront our members with all aspects of social responsibility in the world in which they live and are growing up.

We seek to emphasize the spiritual aspect of education within modern society." "These conversations obviously raise questions about the nature of society and the individual's contribution to it and so can be said to come within your broad definition of political education" (Toc H). Some social educators still identify 'politics' as an enemy — divisive, partisan. "One of our obvious aims is to help members to understand the world in which they are growing up, but no particular emphasis is placed on politics." Other movements, traditionally "social educators", are making a thoughtful and sustained response to the challenge of political education. Prominent among these are the Scouts.[8] The Guides also are beginning to face the challenge as are the Brigades.

Formerly, preparation for citizenship was associated with docility and conformity and not with critical questioning.[9] In the atmosphere of the time, this was inevitable. Educational institutions will always to a degree mirror the prevailing ethos of their societies. It was unlikely that the voluntary youth movements would have sprung up and survived unless prominent among their aims had been the nurture of citizens who were law-abiding, respectful and responsible. Nor should it be assumed that docility was the only purpose even from the first days. Early in the history of these organizations we find the leaders encouraging self-government by young people in their movements and seeking to give them a bigger share in decision-making.[10] Moreover, nobody would wish to deny that the traditional voluntary youth movements — usually associated with the churches — have throughout their history offered a valuable personal and pastoral service to millions of youngsters, combating the effects of poverty, homelessness and educational deprivation, and acting on the belief that many could become fuller personalities and enjoy a more fulfilling life, if they were not just left to themselves.

However, a new intention is abroad today. Calls for docility and deference are seldom heard. The cry now is for young people to have more say in the policy and organization of their own movements. This goes so far as sometimes demanding that youth service should be run entirely by young people themselves. Others would not want to go so far and whilst forfeiting adult control, favour a partnership of power across the generations.[11] Most would agree that the old patterns of youth work are too paternalistic, judged by the standards of our time. It is as though the days of colonialism in the youth service are over and the young are to assume sovereignty in their own territory.

Helped by their own idealistic intentions, the youth organizations of the churches have not been slow to respond to these pressures. Many policy statements, organizational changes and programmes seek to give young people more say in "running their own show" at local, regional and national levels. Social education is seen to involve more than learning how to develop individual gifts, make a satisfying use of leisure time, develop a varied range of personal relationships, and become a responsible citizen. It is seen as including the possibility of acquiring organizational skills, making decisions about the organization to which you belong and acting politically within it.

The current literature of most traditional youth organizations displays a clear and repeated recognition of this aspect of political education. It is the acknowledgement that though the offer of self-government has perhaps been made throughout the history of the movement, yet the practice needs to be up-dated under present circumstances; and that the perpetuation of old practices may unconsciously represent paternalism — which is a benevolent form of authoritarianism — and adult control. Typical of much else written in this sense is *Scouting and the Open Society*. "Successive recountings have now removed from the Scout Law the undertaking to obey the orders of certain persons 'without question' " (p. 41).

Most of the traditional youth organizations are now engaged in the demanding but creative task of discovering how they can hand over more power to the young without destroying their original ethos. In the broadest sense this is an attempt to construct programmes of political education.

All these developments can thus be quoted as examples of the churches' endeavours to forward the political education of the young. There can be no question of the sincerity and value of these interests and plans, whatever the difficulties encountered in practice. But they have one weakness as a mechanism for political education. They tend to accept the present social system too uncritically. They do not conspicuously encourage critical (though not negative) questioning of our whole way of life. In a sense they represent the old docility in a modern dress. They fail to come to terms with the fact that our society will

change radically and therefore they do not invite young people
to think about and take part in these changes. They are not on
the whole designed to help young people involve themselves in a
social revolution, however gentle, gradual and non-violent that
revolution may be. They encourage nonconformity-with-
deference rather than "coming-of-age". Valuable as the efforts
of the "social educators" are, in terms of the James typology,
they are firmly in the category of the "Democratic Preservers".
They make strenuous efforts to involve young people in running
their own movements: but they do not commonly say, "There
may be something seriously wrong with the way this country is
run: and if so you may do a little to improve matters."

Political Educators

There are church-affiliated youth clubs which have faced
squarely and courageously the dilemmas and difficulties of the
political education of the young. They are able to accept that
society at present has unacceptable features leading to
ostentatious wealth and debilitating multi-deprivation; that in a
market economy, some people will even sell the innocence of
their children for gain, as in child pornography. They can invite
their members to consider whether they should enlist in the
struggle against evil that has worked itself into the economic,
political and social systems under which we live.

One illustration is a comment from the Scouts Association.[12]
"Leaders in the Movement are under an obligation to encourage other members to think about social issues of all kinds
including the more controversial items. If leaders ignore issues
which are live and relevant and play 'safe' they do a disservice to
their members. Radical thinking and innovatory projects are
encouraged." That is revolutionary talk in a movement which
draws 58% of its leadership from the managerial and
professional classes.

"As Scouts however we must remain strictly non-political."
It is necessary to make statements of this kind because anything
else would be associated with party political alignment,
partisanship, and even maybe a revolutionary commitment.
Once more we encounter the widespread ambiguity about the
word "political".

Each of the major denominational youth departments has
made substantial forays into the field of political education. If

we compare an agenda for a conference today with one from twenty years ago, we are far more likely to find social and political issues like racism being dealt with. Their literature discloses the same concerns: "So the love of Christ compels us to take action that will seek to improve standards of health, employment, housing, education and political freedom for our fellow workers."[13]

Projects of political education in the Methodist church relate to one of the stated aims of the Methodist Association of Youth Clubs. "Members should be helped to develop a global view of the world in which they live. A church trying to keep young people from contact with the world is doing a grave disservice.[14] Consistent with this objective, the Division of Education and Youth in the Methodist Church issues literature designed to help local groups, organizes conferences with political subjects on the agenda and has schemes for the young in voluntary service overseas.[15] In the Roman Catholic church, the Young Christian Worker's movement has long encouraged discussion of political issues. Vatican statements in recent years have fostered involvement of this kind. "The Catholic Youth Service Council and Diocesan Youth Commissioners have thought it important to engage wherever possible in explicit influence on public policies which shape the context in which young people have to live their lives."[16] This expansion is not widely appreciated either within or outside the church. Even less publicity is received by local groups of young Christians who may be encouraged to act politically as part of their faith commitment. A former Anglican Diocesan Youth Officer writes: "I had a group of young people from different parishes who met regularly and discussed a whole range of issues both concerned with the church and outside. Two young men as a result of this became involved in party politics, one as a Councillor at the age of 22 and another as a Shop Steward also at 22."

These developments represent the nearest approach to a genuine policy of political education in the churches. They do not exclude the possibility that young people will want to question critically the system under which we live: they are not just being recruited for support of the status quo. Such policies and programmes for political education show that these churches are not content to stay with the consensus model of social integration. The old aim of inculcating a variety of "good citizenship'', that could be reduced to acquiescence in existing norms, is no longer accepted. A ''conflict model'' of society is seen as worth considering; it is recognized that political education may involve the young in a struggle to change present practices.

Yet such leaders have to move cautiously, if only out of regard for their public relationship responsibilities. In the present climate, anybody in the churches who uses the conflict model is likely to be judged a Marxist, and therefore godless. Most church members today being middle-class feel threatened by ''revolutionary talk''. They may demand that their leaders ''preach the gospel'' and may withdraw their support if they deem the church is becoming too political. They are looking for a religious fellowship which is above the controversies that are tearing men apart in the world.

Faced with this situation, church leaders are chary of pressing too strongly the case for encouraging the young in ''political action''. Leaders in organizations with democratic pretensions cannot move too far ahead of followers. Moreover, the leaders are working with a youth population not conspicuous for political interest.

So the youth departments of the churches proceed carefully. Indeed, there are indications that having grasped the nettle firmly — having recognized that politics is partly about conflict — they then relinquish their hold. Political education thus becomes a matter of gathering information about other countries whilst avoiding the question of how far those problems arise from an unjust system; of personal service to various groups of the deprived (involvement in which may of course lead to political interest), and attempts to involve the young more actively in the running of their own organizations. So they proceed bravely but carefully into the arena of political conflict.

Excellent as these developments are, they commonly shrink from one commitment: the explicit invitation to young people to consider the possibility that the whole system under which we live might be unjust and contrary to God's will. Of course there are many reasons for this hesitation — pastoral, economic, organizational and ideological — but it cannot be overlooked in any honest assessment of the approaches of organized Christianity to the political education of the young. There is a reluctance to take the Magnificat too seriously. Among the churches therefore, the "political educators" as we have defined them, are those who have bravely assumed the mantle of the "Democratic Transformers" but who under pressure are constantly tempted to become "Democratic Preservers" or "Aristocratic Transformers". Having once faced the possibility that there is something quite seriously wrong with aspects of our present society, having contemplated the possibility that there is at least a grain of truth in the Marxist critique ("though we do not have to swallow it whole"), they then — faced with the expectations of their supporters — feel a gravitational pull towards the goals of personal development, personal service and support of the "Establishment".

Biblical Radicalism

This leaves one more interesting category. It consists of movements which are non-denominational in structure and inter-denominational in membership. They have a clear commitment to the Christian faith but they have greater freedom because they are not tied to the expectations of one particular church. They are free to explore the possibility that Christianity might be a revolutionary faith challenging the present order, and that God is the champion of human rights, the preserver of human dignity and has a special relationship with the poor everywhere. They can offer hospitality to the notion of a radical Christianity, provide a forum where political activists both secular and believing can meet, recognize that membership in protest groups may be a part of Christian obedience and accept that conflict and exploitation are realities without thereby abandoning a Christian view of life for a Marxist perspective.

Chief among these inter-denominational bodies is the Frontier Youth Trust which is associated with the Scripture Union Movement. Many quotations can be provided from their literature illustrating the proposition that Christian discipleship and biblical understanding may involve young disciples in organized attempts radically to change their society. "Make a positive Christian response to alleviate the situation and where possible to change a society that allows such a problem to arise." "The Biblical understanding demands that we reject as demonic any attempt to drive a wedge between evangelism and social action." "God is dishonoured by the reasons for the plight of the needy, the oppressed and the outcast."[17]

In the literature of the Frontier Youth Trust, we have the most forthright, explicit, sustained and thoughtful acknowledgement that Christian obedience may not be fulfilled by acts of personal devotion and personal service alone, but may call for direct political action to establish a system closer to God's ultimate intention of justice and freedom. The literature of the British Council of Churches sounds a similar note.

Most significant in recent years has been the evolution in the thinking and practice of the Scripture Union. They have long been associated with an evangelical outlook based on the authority of the Bible as primarily a book about individual conversion. But now, in a series of booklets and conferences, they have further recognized that the God of the Bible is the God of the nations as well as the Saviour of the soul: that he speaks in mercy and judgement to social and political systems as well as to the sinner. In popular language (which is not entirely accurate) they have discovered that the gospel is also social.[18]

In this area, the dam of political involvement has burst its banks. Only a long survey would describe the activities of Christian agencies dealing with this aspect of youth work. (At the end of chapter five, a list of names and addresses is given). The Student Christian Movement, as well as the British Council of Churches, works in this area; so does the Universities and Colleges Christian Fellowship (formerly Inter-Varsity Fellowship). They recently held their largest student conference (1,400) on the theme "Vocation '78". TEAR Fund, Christian Aid and the youth wings of the missionary societies all have a strong political thrust. The charismatic movement is developing a social/political dimension.[19] The London headquarters of the Mennonites is known as a useful source of information about biblical, political theology.[20]

These movements, ecumenical, inter-denominational, non-denominational, could have an important role in prompting the churches — both at national and local level — to face the issues. This is not only because they are able to pool resources, but also because they have more freedom in the matter, being less subject than the denominations to the pressures which often arise from a bourgeois orientation or the pious expectations of those who, expecting total salvation to come "from above", are not interested in the "politics of the valley".

The pity is that so far as I can see — and to return to an earlier theme — the understanding of the gospel represented in these last two categories has made little impact on educational practice in local churches. It has of course proved much more difficult to secure reliable evidence in this area. To read the policy statements of the churches is a simple matter but to gain any clear picture of what is the general practice on the "shop-floor" of the church, is well-nigh impossible. I have to rely on two sources. One is my observations of the practice in local churches over several years. The other is the response to my issuing a wide invitation through many journals for local Christian groups to send me accounts of how they attempted to provide political education, in the broadest terms, for young people. From both sources the resultant picture is discouraging. Local churches do not include in their programmes for the young an intention to help them even to think — much less to act — politically.

(Over the last two years, my research into political education among Christian youth groups has doubly surprised me. First at how much is being thought and done at a national, international, non-denominational and inter-denominational level; but secondly at the ample confirmation of my worst fears that apparently little is being done in the local church and among the members of single units of Christian youth organizations).

In the worst cases, far from being prepared to live in the world as Christians, the young are invited to withdraw from it, at least once a week. Worship and ritual occur in a separate theatre. A sentimental "gospel" is offered which in essence consists of affirming that God loves you and there is hence no cause for dismay. In such places the leaders do not encourage the young to think and act for themselves. Young people are invited to join a middle-class ghetto, not God's army of "Democratic Transformers". They are mobilized for social stability, seldom for social change.

This is not to deny that the local church often fulfils an important pastoral role for the young person: much effort goes into encouraging the personal growth and development of individual young people. Equally, nobody should underestimate the value of voluntary community service which the churches inspire among their younger members, both within and beyond the organization of the church. But these efforts tend to be of a "personal service" kind with little attempt to think through social and political implications: their efforts leave them politically innocent. The young are encouraged to visit the old, decorate their rooms and dig their gardens, but not to ask questions about a society which creates vast disparities of wealth. They visit hospital wards, bringing cheer to the patients, perhaps conducting a service, but they are not prompted to ask why the National Health Service is hampered by lack of funds. Such enterprises produce helpful people who think of the needs of others — a consequence that is not to be despised. But they do not of themselves develop persons who have "come of age and have a mind of their own".

Typical of this approach — both in splendour and short-comings — is one church where, under inspiring leadership, the young people have been involved in a number of useful projects with an international reference. They have helped to buy a tractor for an agricultural community in a poor African country and earned the money to dig a well in an India village. But none of these experiences have been used to develop understanding of the economic, social and political features of the human situation they have worked to improve. (It is as though in the churches we work with the unconscious assumption that the religious impulse absolves us from the necessity of grappling with the political realities, as though our faith gives us a licence to by-pass the mechanics of change. In the local church there is frequently a conspiracy of silence about political realities, just as, it is said, there used to be a similar conspiracy about sex.)

By contrast with this admittedly heartening example of practical concern for others, I set one of the few examples I have discovered where a church youth group is encouraged to come to terms with the political facts of our situation. This is what happens in the St. Andrew's Methodist Centre, Halifax. The programme is balanced in two senses. First, it attempts a mixture of thought and action. Significantly, their broadsheet[21] on political education was in wide demand throughout the country. It does not avoid the "conflict" issue: one chapter is headed "The advantages and disadvantages of capitalism". Every Tuesday night during the past five years, a "chat shop" has been attended by about 20-25 members and addressed by a guest speaker. Recent subjects have been Racism,

Unemployment, Trade Unions, Disarmament and the Third World. As for action— the youth worker, Ken Fleming, also encourages the club members to take part in campaigns on political issues about which they feel keenly, like apartheid and world poverty. The second important element is that young people are offered the opportunity of acting politically both on their own and others' behalf. "Decision making by young people is a priority at St. Andrews and we have managed to get young people represented not only on our management committees but on the various education policy-making commitees".[22]

If the church is to be more politically aware and active, to take its place amongst those resisting bureaucracy, injustice, tyranny, and to oppose all forms of organized dehumanization, then we must look for an improvement in the weekly diet of worship, training and action in local churches. We should also remember that it is likely to be more productive if we present perspectives to the young rather than to older people. The following paragraphs attempt to draw together the threads of this chapter and to summarize the argument for additional approaches in the programmes of local churches.

1. We repeat that the issue is primarily theological: it concerns the picture of God which is presented in local churches. The whole case rests on a conviction that the God who is revealed in the Bible cares about social righteousness as well as individual salvation. We are faithless if we allow this prophetic dimension to drop out. If the biblical picture of God is true, then it is in the church where he is proclaimed in his fulness that we have the best hope of bringing together the pastoral and the political understanding of the human situation. The God who raised Jesus from the dead saves us both from an individualism which makes us forget the historical process and from a preoccupation with the historical process which renders the individual insignificant.

2. Local congregations should hear more about the activities of Christianity as a world movement, not forgetting those Christians who fight political tyranny in Latin America and South Africa. At present most of the folk heroes of local congregations are dead; their lives were entirely devoted to their personal relationship with God, the conversion of individual souls and the support of the church. While we hear more

frequently about the troubles of the religious dissidents in Russia, this topic is more acceptable to congregations since *they* are fighting against Communism. Many local churches need to be moved from an automatic identification with social stability.

3. None of this means that the local church should abandon its central pastoral concern for individuals, and their growth and development, in the context of a Christian understanding of life. This concern must remain its strength and glory: the local church personalizes the gospel: it embodies that love of God which counts the hairs on our heads and notices when a single sparrow falls to the ground. What is demanded is simply an updating of the churches' pastoral care for the young. Youth work is effective when it represents a response to the present needs of young people. And today, as never before, human lives are affected by politics so that caring for young people now includes paying attention to the political dimension of their lives. The old goals of fulfilment and self-realization are to be seen partly in the light of political awareness. The judgement of God requires that local churches seek to be both pastorally and politically effective.

4. Political education is not limited to national and international affairs. It also concerns the many associations to which each of us belongs — family, church, youth club, school, local community. So it is quite proper that political education should teach us about our own rights and how to secure them, about courteously standing up for ourselves and our social group. As a pastor I frequently encountered cases where bureaucratic officials dispensed cavalier treatment to people who were unable to stand up for themselves often because they did not already know their rights, were not told about those rights and further lacked the confidence to resist pressure from officialdom. Christ has many things to teach us, and one is to discard the old docility and deference and believe in our own God-given dignity. The ugly word "conscientization" arose from the work of Paolo Freire in Brazil.[23] It combines two realities. The first is "consciousness" — an awareness of your own situation and how this has been created by the actions of other people, capitalists and others. The second is "conscience" — the understanding that what is wrong in your situation is wrong in God's sight and demands change. "Conscientization" should be one benefit of church membership. It is proper that political educa-

tion should motivate young people to be aware of their own
rights and confer dignity and self-confidence to resist bureaucracy and injustice. Christian meekness is not be be confused
with docility and deference. Claiming your own political rights
can often be the preliminary to working for the political emancipation of others. Ken Fleming of St. Andrew's Methodist
Youth Centre tells how the effect of political education in his
club prompted the members to organize themselves and act
politically on their own behalf. Once he received a directive
from the local authority that members' subscriptions were to be
increased by 100%. The club had no need of extra money and in
fact subscriptions were kept down by a system of quarterly and
annual payments. But in the club, where political education is a
recognized part of the programme, the members were not
prepared to accept without question this ruling from on high.
They wrote to object, as did fifty parents. In the end, the
increase was reduced to a modest 10%. On another occasion,
the authority, as an economy measure, decided to close the club
during August, when many members are on holiday and most
need its facilities. The club representative on the Youth
Advisory committee was briefed to question the decision: the
following year the club was allowed to open in August. But
what happens to young people who lack the training and the
confidence to act politically on their own behalf?

A Christian youth group having political education may not
be prepared to accept unquestioningly decisions made by church
authorities affecting their organizations. This may cause
conflict, but if the opposition is conducted courteously and
fairly, it would be a matter of rejoicing that they are growing up
in Christ, passing from the status of slaves to that of sons and
daughters.

5. But political education is far more than learning the skills
to gain justice for yourself and your group. (Although this is
how it is projected in some secular circles where political
education simply equals political action for your own group
interests.) But the Gospel — like other faiths — adds another
dimension to political interest and activity. It prompts us to act
on behalf of others. One looks for the day when it is normative
for young Christians to belong to political groups as part of
their discipleship. "What will you do for God and Man now
that you have become a Christian?" Prominent among present

answers to that question are, "Become a Sunday School teacher/youth worker/evangelist." Perhaps in the future answers might more freqently refer to joining movements like Shelter or Child Poverty.

6. Action must be a marked feature of the churches' programmes of political education. It is for "average" children as well as those who are highly gifted academically. Today there is a serious threat that local congregations will be largely composed of an educated élite. This is cause for concern, not because one group is superior but because those who can handle abstract concepts and learn much from books, and those who usually learn from doing and experience, have so much to give to each other. "Political education" must be more than a subject of debate, a kind of additional A level in informal education. Based on his world-wide experience, Ian Fraser[24] has shown us that one test of a sound theology is how effective it is in facilitating social change.

7. What has been written so far may give the impression that the choices are more clear-cut than in fact they are: we may have been over-simplifying the issue. But difficult decisions must be made on several fronts; only practice and experimentation can resolve our problems, as groups of Christians try to work out together what it means to follow Christ on the contemporary scene. But this attempt will itself be an adventure and for many of us will add a new dimension of excitement and reality to our obedience.

At the outset, we face the problem that we cannot invite the young to share a blue-print of Christian political involvement. There are still too many unanswered questions in this area. For example — are Christians simply to support all "liberal" measures or is there a distinctively Christian political perspective?

A more immediate question is: "What should be our attitude to the existing political structures?" There are signs that for many young people the professional politicians have largely lost credibility; they are looking to, and associating with, political movements outside the mainstream of organized political life. The reasons for this discontent are understandable. Major political parties give the impression of having no policies which can match the inevitable changes and the new problems which face mankind. (Karl Jaspers has identified the present time as a period when history turns so that things can never quite be the same again). They go on mouthing their futile old-fashioned nostrums which are seen to be increasingly irrelevant in a world threatened by the stock-piling of arms, the destruction of the environment and the growth of population. For mass unemployment, largely created by technological advances, they offer cosmetic treatment when only a new style of living is adequate. Is it any wonder that many young people conclude that politics is too serious a matter to be left to the politicians and that some have decided that the existing political machinery is not adequate for the changes which must now be sought by direct action? In this confusion, one thing is clear. Any suggestion (sometimes made) that there can be only one party for Christians to join is quite ludicrous. A more pertinent question is whether there is any large party where the Christian can look for the fulfilment of his hopes. The present political parties are there; they are likely to be on the scene for a long time; they represent a large part of the constitutional machinery for effecting social change through Parliament.

What older and younger Christians might discuss in local churches is their duty to give a critical allegiance to that party which in their view holds out the strongest hope for movement towards justice and freedom. They cannot give an absolute commitment to any party, but they should recognize their obligation as Christians to join in organized action.

Recently, Thomas and Roberts[25] explained why we cannot be satisfied with the programmes of any of the major political parties since they are not addressing themselves to contemporary problems — yet we cannot simply turn our backs on them, since they are there and have power. We should join the party of our choice but once inside constantly ask questions: What about: Sharing existing jobs? . . . A shorter working week, more time at home? . . . Reviving rural life? . . . Education at all ages? . . . Linking disarmament to Third World development? . . . Neighbourhood community forums for community affairs?

Thomas and Roberts were not writing specifically with Christians in mind. Yet looking at these questions and this kind of commitment, one feels that this is the way in which we may fulfil our mission to go into the secular situation listening for the word of God, to help the church to become "multi-

political" not merely "non-political", and to harness to contemporary issues the moral and spiritual power generated in the
churches. The political parties too would benefit from this style
of commitment, though Christians in this situation may be wise
to refer only rarely to the source of their critique — the word of
God.

8. In all this pleading, it is necessary to sound a cautionary
word. We must not raise unrealistic hopes about the power of
young people to change the world. It is the custom of some to
offer the political involvement of young people as a panacea for
all our ills. That way lies disappointment and disillusionment.
The walls of Jericho will not fall at a single shout from teen-
agers. Older people fail the young when they suggest that there
are easy solutions for complicated conflicts like that between
Arabs and Jews in the Middle East or Protestants and Catholics
in Northern Ireland. This feeds those fantasies to which many
of us are prone when young. But political education may
persuade us that we can do something on a smaller scale, that
this something is worth doing and that we are not just pawns in
a gigantic game of chess that is being played by the world rulers.
In the immediate situation, we can work for political justice.
And when we can do nothing to change political injustice, we
may work to diminish the effects of dehumanization. That is the
role of many Christian community workers in Northern Ireland.
They have no immediate political solution that is likely to be
accepted for the troubles but they are helping many people to
remain human in an atmosphere of violence. And at least they
appreciate the political aspect of the troubles and do not
attribute them all to individual wickedness. It may well be that if
a local church included programmes of political education, the
young people would still be chiefly engaged on those valuable
acts of personal service which are common today. But now they
would perform them with a growing appreciation of the political dimension of the situation of those whom they seek to
serve. As to the larger national and international issues, Christian responses mean that we are helping the slow advent of a new
climate of public opinion in which new political solutions are
possible. So, the concentration of churches in Northern Ireland
on individual relationships across the divide is not politically
irrelevant. The results are long-delayed: there is a constant
temptation to lose heart and abandon the attempt. But the

hopes of Christians in these endeavours are continuously re-inforced by the God of hope.

This chapter represents a vision whereby the local church may involve its members in struggles for political justice and freedom. It seeks to describe an engagement in politics from a distinctively Christian standpoint whilst still respecting the "secular" realities of the political situation. It is an invitation to listen for God's word and do God's will in a world where men struggle for the possession and control of scarce resources.

If these ideas are right, how may they be given legs? The last chapter offers practical suggestions for programmes of political education for the young in churches.

5
Methods of Political Education

There can be no blue-print for programmes of political education in local Christian youth groups. This is a good thing, for the impossibility reflects the *educational* nature of the task. We cannot impose a pattern from above. Our intention is to offer opportunities whereby young people have the chance of becoming politically mature and literate adults. If our aim is to offer some of the means by which young people can gain their freedom, then we must strive to make our means consistent with the ends.

There can be no standardized programmes because local situations vary greatly. The age of the members, the resources we have, notably in manpower, the type of neighbourhood where we work — all these are part of that reality which is as sacred as the gospel.

Moreover, politics should not usually be treated as a separate subject. It is better seen as part of our understanding of the human situation, helping to form the relationship which develops between adult workers and adolescent members. Awareness of the political dimension of life should run through the total life of the group, like the name "Blackpool" through the rock.[1] Politics is not something to be dragged in on special occasions. (That would be reminiscent of the old type club epilogue which sought "to bring God into the club" as though he had not been there all the evening!) Effective political education is rooted in the worker's inner respect for each member, in his willingness to listen, to provide experiences when appropriate, to respond to needs — and if it is not rooted in these realities it cannot be stuck on in special sessions. For Christians, political education will take place in a context of caring for the growing development and fulfilment of individuals — it is an extension of our traditional pastoral and educational functions.

Eli is still the archetypal figure for Christians who work with young people in voluntary associations.[2] But Eli offered help only when Samuel was perplexed, and the youngster was left to make his own response.

This thought suggests a priority of Christian groups are to essay programmes of political education. First, as the admirable Mrs. Beeton wrote, catch your hare. Find the adults who have the interest and the outlook to engage in this enterprise and the willingness to increase their knowledge and enhance their skill through further training.

The best place to begin is not always the most obvious. Four days in Calcutta depressed me unutterably. It is a "corner of hell". Nowhere is human suffering and deprivation so poignant. Eventually I was shown into the office of the principal Welfare Officer. "Where would you begin," he asked, "with problems of this magnitude? Don't say birth control or education." I could see he wanted to tell me and anyway I was in despair! "The most practical thing you could do for Calcutta is to build another bridge." Even I, with my brief acquaintance with the city and its problems, could see the sense of it. Nine million people have only one bridge across the River Hooghly in twenty miles. Another bridge would relieve the congestion and spread the population through the surrounding countryside. Similarly with present aspirations — we start at a point that may not be the most obvious; not with the programmes themselves, but with the men and women who may sponsor them. This judgement is confirmed by my enquiries. Wherever in a church youth group I have found programmes aiming at political literacy, there has been at least one adult in the background whose enthusiasm has been decisive. Significantly, my enquiries have brought me into touch with many more who feel they ought and would like to include the fostering of political literacy among their objectives, but who feel they lack the knowledge, ability, or confidence to begin. Many in the church have the will but lack the skill in this affair.

Political educators in the church will be men and women who

understand that the gospel sends us out into the "secular" world to listen there for God's word and to fulfil our mission there. They realize that God is not saving the world through the efforts of the church alone, but that the Christian is there to interpret to the world God's saving activity in the world outside the church; and they appreciate that the facts of the political situation are no less sacred than the truth of the gospel. With the young people themselves, they will know that their prime function is not to persuade them of "the truth", but to help the young people, where they can, to come of age, think and decide for themselves as individuals and members of a society. Such adults will be flexible, ready to play different roles as required by the developing needs of the young — information-givers, resource-persons, encouragers, and representatives of the demand of excellence.

To this formidable list two requirements should be added. They will probably have to be people of quiet courage, able courteously to sustain their convictions. For the evidence suggests that any Christian youth worker who undertakes programmes of political education will encounter opposition from "the authorities" and from the adult members of the congregation, some of it based on a misunderstanding of his intentions.[3] Such Christian youth workers must also be ready to undergo some further training in this area — probably on a part-time basis — by means of courses which one hopes will increasingly be made available by church organizations. To complete the picture, these courses should have well-marked features, some of which we have learned in recent years from training processes which are primarily aimed at the improvement of skill rather than the acquisition of knowledge.

(i) *The experimental approach:* students will have experiences which prompt reflection, assessment and analysis rather than being given chunks of knowledge in books and lectures. For all skill training, a Chinese proverb is highly pertinent: "What I hear, I forget: what I see, I remember: what I do, I know".

(ii) *The contents of the course* will cover three broad fields: (a) Access to the information required to support programmes of political education in Christian groups. (b) Exploration of the attitudes and values of political educators who work within the context of a Gospel view of man, society and the world. (c) Practice in the skills of political education.

(iii) *They should offer the student support for his own personal development,* which is an important matter for the political educator. This often means for example, re-interpreting his own past experiences.

A matter of prime importance for national church organizations is communication. There are today many exciting developments in the Christian world. There has been an explosion of biblical theology, which has destroyed many of our old pietistic sanctions. We see Christian groups long associated with a stress on individual holiness now becoming aware of the political dimension of the gospel. We have "Christian freedom-fighters" in many lands. Yet it is common to find that news of these developments has not reached the local church and the local youth unit and its leaders. One of the saddest features of my researches has been to find some local Christian youth workers who want to help their members to be politically literate yet feel terribly isolated with these hopes. Somehow they have dropped through the elaborate network of communications which undoubtedly exists. Too often people simply do not know what is happening in this area. There can be no substantial progress until the parishioners of Much-Binding-in-the-Marsh have the opportunity to feel that the priests who oppose apartheid in South Africa and tyranny in Latin America are their blood brothers. The churches must attend to the mechanics of communicating contemporary Christian involvement.

Turning to specific programmes in local units, there are one or two general points to be made, some of which gather up the arguments in previous sections. Such programmes should not be "tacked on" to the rest of the activities, but consistent with them. They are intended to be an expression of a pastoral and educational process where our primary aim is for the young people to come of age. They are to be part of a group atmosphere where members feel they are valued for their own sake, where they are tempted to engage in new activities and constantly challenged by standards of excellence, where there is an attentive adult ear if they want to speak into it and where they have a hand in the running of their own show.

The programmes throughout will take an experiential approach; they will seek to root political education in the present experience of the individual, as being at the receiving end of political decisions, a member of society, where a struggle is taking place for the control and use of scarce resources. Most of us begin to be aware of political realities by first becoming aware of our own political situation and possibilities. But the programmes are based on the hope that we shall want to move beyond ourselves, to be politically literate about the world in which we are growing up. When we come to these wider matters, we must remember the point that has been driven home again and again by members of the Hansard Society and the Politics Association.[4] We begin with issues and move to concepts, not the other way round: not with "justice" but with what we mean when we say the referee's decision was "not fair": not with "a fair distribution of the world's wealth" but with pictures of a boy in Calcutta who lives on less than 10p a day, sleeps on the pavement and does not attend school.

From particular examples such as these, we can develop a literacy which will enable us to grasp the structures, processes and ideas of politics.

In what follows, it has been found convenient to place political literacy under several headings — Awareness, Information, Attitudes, Skill and Action. Each section contains activities deemed particularly appropriate to the objective. But these exercises may have a relevance to the other objectives. Equally, there are some exercises which relate to most or all of the objectives. In some local units, I have discovered that there is a weekly "natter session" about current affairs (usually attended by only a minority of the members). This kind of session, whether formal or informal, would encourage awareness, increase knowledge, foster attitudes, teach skills and prompt action.

It hardly needs to be said that not all these exercises are possible in every situation.

Awareness

For many of us creating awareness will be the primary task. We are simply not fully aware of the fact that we live our lives in a "political envelope". Many of us say that we are "not interested in politics", to which the rejoinder might be that politics is interested in us. There are parallels in the rest of our experience. We may not be aware of the circulatory system within our bodies though the blood has always been coursing through our veins. When Paul came to Ephesus he heard people within the local Christian community confess that they did not know whether there was a Holy Spirit, yet if Paul's gospel was right, the Spirit was part of their daily experience. Does it matter if we are not aware of the realities — psychological, political, spiritual — in which we live and move and have our being? Some would say it is not important to know. Life is for living not for understanding. Others insist that it is always better for humans to know than not to know; that we should have our eyes opened even to look at a painful world — that to be aware is to be human. And in political matters, unless we are ready to go through a process of "conscientization" whereby we come to comprehend our human situation, we are more likely to be slaves, subject to tyranny, oppression and injustice, not free men and women. The main purpose of "political awareness" is not to produce more political savants and activists, for generally they will be in a minority, it is rather to help us all to understand better our own human situation. Politics impinges on our private lives. To grasp that is one condition of knowing ourselves. We may even have to defend our private lives from the intrusion of politics. Political educators, by the nature of their task, are compelled to agree that it is better, more human, to know than not to know.

Stated in these terms, learning awareness sounds a dull pursuit. In fact, it can be one of the most enjoyable and exciting parts of the programme. For we can begin to acquire political awareness by playing games which turn out to be great fun.

One such game is called "Star Power"[5], now widely used on courses of leadership training. The main object of this game is to give the participants some experience of what it feels like to be part of a group where each member has a different degree of power (not of their own choosing) and no individual can exercise much control over what happens to him; a political experience within a game.

The following will be needed:

— At least twenty players, divided, as nearly as possible, into three equally-sized groups.

— A large room, so that the groups cannot easily overhear each other.

— A large number of tiddley winks, to be known as "counters": red, green, black,, white and brown.

— Enough badges, one for each player. The badges to be

squares, circles and triangles. Whichever badge a player receives identifies him with his group.

The game proceeds as follows: each player is given five counters. The values of the counters are:

Red — 50 points; Green — 25 points; Black — 15 points; White — 10 points; Brown — 5 points.

Members of the square group are given one red counter, one green counter and three random counters from black, white or brown. Members of the circle group are given one green and four random counters from the black, white and brown. Members of the triangle group are given five random counters from the black, white and brown. One member of the circle group and one member of the triangle group are each given counters to the same value as one of the members of the square group.

   (i) Ten minutes to improve your score.
  (ii) Scores are improved by trading advantageously with other squares, triangles and circles.
 (iii) Only one-for-one trades are legal. Two-for-one or any other combinations are illegal.
  (iv) Persons must be holding hands to effect a trade.
   (v) Once you touch the hand of another participant a chip of unequal value or colour must be traded. If a couple cannot consummate a trade they may have to hold hands for the entire ten minutes trading session.
  (vi) No talking unless hands are touching.
 (vii) Persons with folded arms do not have to trade with other persons.
(viii) All chips must be hidden.
  (ix) Value of chips
       Red   50 — 5 chips of same colour — extra 25
       Green 25 — 4 chips of same colour — extra 15
       Black 15 — 3 chips of same colour — extra 10
       White 10 — 3 chips of same colour — extra 0
       Brown 5

Players are told not to show their counters to anybody else, in their own or other groups, and are not given a list of the bargaining rules which are as follows:

The players believe that the aim is to improve their score by bargaining from the same assets and they do not realize at this stage that they have been given counters of differing value. After ten minutes of trading according to the rules, everybody is asked to add up the points in their hand and the scores are put on the blackboard in each group. Those with high scores are praised and those with low scores are blamed or ridiculed. At this stage it is obvious that the members of the square group have done very well and only one member in each of the other groups has done well.

Each group is then given three yellow counters worth twenty points each which they can give to or distribute among one, two, or three members of their group as they like. When this has been done the scores of the individuals who have benefited are altered on the board.

Now the groups are re-allocated. Those with the highest scores become the square group: it will probably be much the same as the old square group but with one or two high scores from the other two groups. Those with the lowest scores become the triangle group; again, it will probably be much the same as the old triangle group but with some changes. The rest, in the middle range, become the circle group.

With the re-groupings, the whole process can be repeated for as many sessions as there is time for and so long as interest is retained. But at some point, the person in charge 'rewards' the square group for their high scoring by allowing them to make the rules for subsequent bargaining.

After a time (sometimes as early as the second bargaining session) the players begin to realize that they have been given a 'poor hand' to start with and this begins to affect the way they play. For example, they may cheat, opt out, or try to infiltrate the square group; sometimes the two 'bottom groups' will combine against the square group. In making the rules the 'squares' are usually very dictatorial but they may try to create a more egalitarian system. In other words, left to themselves, the players will try out all sorts of possibilities and solutions thus reflecting the patterns in real life, and creating a microcosmic political system. *It is important therefore that at the end of the game players spend a fair amount of time looking at what has happened and why.* For some in the group this may be the first experience of belonging to a deprived group; for others it will be an interpretation of their daily experience which they will come to understand better. Very often the frustrations experienced make more impact than any reading on the subject might achieve

Is this any more than a game, exciting and often boisterous?

Bill Cockell has described the three stages which participants commonly experience: (i) This is a joke, I will go along with it. (ii) I am a bit involved but it's only a game. (iii) I really mind about what is happening.

It is when we reflect upon the third stage that the game contributes to our political awareness, opening our eyes to the fact that however else we relate to each other, we are also in competition and that is a large part of what politics is about. Life is partly a struggle for various forms of power and success feeds our ego and prestige.

There are more serious and demanding forms of the "play-approach" which can be used. Some of them may be found in a B.B.C. publication.[6] Another possibility is to use some of the case-studies provided, say by T. R. Batten, of dilemmas with political implications, and work together on what should be done next.[7]

Christian leaders have another opportunity to help increase the political awareness of those whom they seek to serve. In many places today specific Christian teaching based on the Bible is still offered to church youth groups in the Senior Sunday School, the Young People's Fellowship or the Boys' Brigade Bible Class. We can point to the political dimension of the stories used by these groups. This is not a gimmick nor an attempt to be fashionable. It is simply an attempt to recover the first meaning of the original incident. For many of the leaders in the Old Testament the political were inseparable from the religious tasks. Moses discovered his people under oppression, compelled to make bricks without straw. He founded a brick-makers' union and inspired a resistance movement which brought his people to freedom. Elijah, too, was well understood by the authorities of his time to be a freedom-fighter and was instructed by God to act politically. Were Amos alive today, he would probably be a member of the socialist Tribune Group. As John Robinson has reminded us, the response Yahweh seeks from Israel is decision for the God who acts, and decision for the neighbour — the poor and the stranger, the fatherless and the widow. "Again, for the Prophets, no more than for Moses, was politics an affair of this world, a distraction from religion . . . Here right politics is religion: it is what to know the God of history means."[8] To be faithful to the Old Testament we should have to re-write much of the teaching material of the churches. At present, by draining them of their political life, those red-blooded men are turned into anaemic nonentities.

But is politics as important in the New Testament as in the Old? Certainly the circumstances have changed, and the Sermon on the Mount has fulfilled and replaced the Ten Commandments. But political realities remain, simply because they are always part of the human situation. We forget this when for example we give a wholly supernatural interpretation to the death of Jesus and overlook the fact that he was crucified largely because his teaching and ministry deeply challenged the contemporary political powers. He too was seen as a freedom fighter by the authorities. "The whole burden of Jesus' message, which he can support to its end only by his death, is precisely the coming of the Kingdom of God into history. And that throws him willy-nilly, as the bearer of the Kingdom, into the very midst of the political struggle, to the extent of being hanged between two insurrectionists — to all the world as one more of them."[9] Today if we imagine that we can respond to Christ's call always and only by personal kindness, we are being escapist. The picture of Jesus that we present to the young in churches can properly include the political dimension of his cause.

Information

If we are to be politically literate we need information and this information should be provided in an assimilable form. Most of us accept facts only if they correspond to our interest and need. That is why the most frequent form of political education in a youth group should be that commonest and choicest activity — talking. Without growing didactic, conversation with individuals and groups offers the worker his best opportunity of political education. To say that the members are interested only in pop music and soccer is often a counsel of despair and an abdication from the position of adult guidance. The function of youth workers is not to impose their own interests and values on members, but it may sometimes be to help those members to discover within themselves unsuspected interests that lie deeply buried. It is in conversation that the need for further information arises both about politics themselves and particular issues that are prominent in the news as well as in our own immediate political situation. Of course, it goes without saying that older people also need this information. Obviously this approach does not exclude other methods, which, clearly, should be discussed with and agreed by the members.

(i) *Leave suitable literature around the place.* It must be in plain, lucid language and give a fair-minded, not propagandist, version of the issues. *Action through the young political parties* and *Action through your M.P.* are two suitable pamphlets published by Anti-Poverty Ltd.

(ii) *Visit projects or organizations which are engaged on enterprises having a political content.* A selection can be made from the list at the end of this chapter. Many of them will have local branches but in addition there will be pressure groups whose activities are confined to the area.[10] It is on those visits that the leader learns to be protective but not over-protective. An opportunity must be given to talk over the experience and it is in the assessment session that one learns how susceptible young people can be to the enthusiasm and propaganda of others. One must resist the temptation to say things like — "But he was not being quite honest at this point", although one may say on the appropriate occasion, "What did you make of — ?" We must not try to rescue them prematurely, which is horribly patronizing. We must believe that they themselves are capable of separating the truth from the propaganda.

(iii) *"Protective but not over-protective."* This is a canon which also applies when we invite visitors to come to the unit and talk about their aspirations and activities. Whether the whole group encourages a particular enthusiast should be decided not by the revolutionary nature of his views but whether he will respect the integrity of his audience and not exploit their youth and lack of experience by a propagandizing approach. On these occasions the worker's intervention is justified to ensure that the visitor will not make a long boring speech; that if possible he brings some audio-visual aids; that he can capture interest when he speaks; and that he can answer questions in a brief, lucid and fair-minded way. Again, the list at the end of the chapter provides suggestions though it gives no clue to the suitability or quality of the visitors and must be tested locally.

(iv) Our concern is specifically with political education in a Christian context. Therefore with some groups it would be legitimate to present *material showing how Christians are acting politically,* notably in countries where they are fighting oppression from the extreme left or the extreme right. Films are one good method.[11] Sometimes there is the right person around, an ex-patriate or a Britisher who has spent a long time in the country concerned. Again one must be chary of inviting the blinkered propagandist.

Attitudes

I hope it is not necessary at this stage to say that specifying certain "attitudes" does not imply that there is an orthodoxy in these matters which must be conveyed by methods subtle or obvious. This book has an emphatic commitment to the view that the Kingdom Christ proclaims has political as well as individual implications. But that is not "a new orthodoxy" — it is a view which is to be subject to the most rigorous scrutiny along with the rest.

"Attitudes" suggests something else. It indicates what have have been called the procedural values of political activity — things like fair-mindedness, tolerance, respect for truth and each other. We learn these best together in small groups. It is no use the Christian worker being an enthusiast for democracy if everybody — except perhaps himself — knows that in discussion he is an authoritarian bully who takes an unfavourable view of those who disagree with his cherished convictions. To listen seriously to the evidence against your views, to act on your convictions whilst admitting that you may conceivably be wrong, to support majority decisions when the issue has been fairly debated — these are the stuff of positive political attitudes. Normally they are learned slowly and in the small group.

Events in the life of the group also provide material for learning political attitudes. Money is regularly stolen from the canteen takings. How shall we deal with this matter? Do we: (1) Accept it as a tolerable level of stealing? (2) Say we think we know who the culprit is so we will exclude him from the canteen counter? (3) Close the canteen for a period? (4) Have only adult helpers in the canteen? (5) Leave the decision entirely to the adult worker? Under effective guidance, members may learn a lot about political attitudes as they face incidents like that. In fact, the process may be more valuable than the product, the learning more important than the decisions. For in a micro-situation we are facing the problem of large societies. How can we protect the interests of the whole without withdrawing the freedom of the individual? How can we have law and order without a fascist régime or at least a police state? The sensitive political educator will not miss the opportunities for acquiring creative political attitudes.

And of course, the youth group itself is a political unit. Effective leaders are always prompting the members to play a more effective part in the decisions of the group, responsibly to accept power. If we promote political action outside the group, wiithout encouraging self-government within it, we are propagandists, not educators. (Conversely, if political education is confined to the group and does not relate to the world outside, we are insular.)

Skill

This section deals with opportunities for young people to learn how to act politically on their own behalf thus involving them in the acquisition of organizational skills. A genuine youth worker understands that part of his function is to prompt and help young people to think and act for themselves in a way that takes account of the rights of others.

Many and varied are the points of contact and need. Tom has started work in a local factory. Does he know what his rights are as an industrial worker? He has had to join a trade union. Is it merely a matter of paying his dues because he is compelled or does he have a bigger view of the rôle of the trade union and the part he might play if he wants to? He wishes to join an art class at the college of further education but is told the class is full and there can be no additional classes on account of economy cuts in the educational budget. Tom says he knows six other fellows in the same position. Do they simply have to accept this decision or can they try to change the decision? And if they are to work to change it, where do they begin? How can they acquire the organizational skills required?

Tom belongs to other groups — home, church, club — which are political in the sense that they have a structure of power and decisions are taken by others which affect his experience. Does he have to accept these decisions unquestioningly though he may be smouldering with resentment about some of them? How can he organize with others in like circumstances, to question and perhaps to change them? This is not to be interpreted narrowly as "group selfishness". In the present Christian context it may be an aspect of Tom's dignity as a son of God. Many who begin by acting politically on their own behalf move on to the next stage where they act politically on behalf of others. There are increasing opportunities in this area today. The British Youth Council[12] and the National Council for Voluntary Youth Services[13] are actively encouraging the setting up of local youth councils. Membership is restricted to those under 26 and where it exists the local council provides a forum where issues affecting young people can be discussed and action on their behalf can be planned.

Action

The word "action" is used here to describe the efforts of young people, either as individuals or in groups, to take part in the life of the community and to work with others to effect what is considered to be necessary change. The report of the Youth Service Development Council[14] saw this as one of the ideal intentions of Youth Service. "In a country such as ours, subject to the changes consequent upon a rapidly developing technology, society needs to engage in an intensive and perpetual transformation of itself, unless it is to respond to tomorrow's world with yesterday's activities and modes of organization . . . Furthermore, the young have the energy and aspirations untrammelled by past failure to secure some parts of the transformation of society which their elders are not necessarily better qualified to achieve."[15] Though this statement has often been criticized as unrealistic, it received some support from the research of Professor John Eggleston of Keele University. He found that though young people were not on the whole characterized by radicalism, they yet showed a marked preference for associating with those movements which — like Shelter — aimed at change rather than stability.

The duty of the Christian youth worker in this matter is clear. He must be a channel of information for individuals and groups as required. (At the end of this chapter, arranged topically, is a list of relevant organizations.) And in response to need, he ought to be ready to help organize the involvement, make necessary contacts and, not least, prompt a critical assessment of the work of the movements.

In this area we should not despise the opportunities for personal service provided for young people by organizations like PHAB, VSO, CSO and "Time for God" (details and a fuller list are given of pages   ). The Involvement with these movements not only provides valuable help for those who need it and is usually "good" for those who give the service, it can also be useful from the present point of view. Such involvement, alerting the young Christians to the facts about the casualities in society may prompt them to think about the underlying causes and thence to ask questions that are specifically political.

Projects

In a few cases, there is the possibility of a generic approach to the political education of the young which can aim at all the goals listed in this chapter. This consists of the group agreeing to act on one specific issue and planning a campaign. There is a fairly lengthy period of preparation in which the participants find that their political awareness is sharpened, their stock of political information is increased and their skill enhanced.

One example of such an enterprise was when a youth group mounted a successful campaign to change the decision of the local council to withdraw the free bus passes of pensioners for reasons of economy.

A Christian youth club in Maidstone, Kent, initiated two enterprises of this kind. In the first, twenty young people staged a demonstration in the centre of Maidstone to ask people to "Sign in on World Poverty". In the second, seven club members and two leaders joined the national "Stop the 70 Tour Committee" when the M.C.C. had invited an all-white cricket team to tour this country.[16]

Conclusion

The task of the Christian youth worker as political educator is not easy: aspects of it are even frightening and forbidding. He will encounter many perplexities. What is he to say, for example, when a group of his members consider joining the Anti-Nazi League and seek his advice? But the present argument is that for the Christian political educator there are always growth points in a continuing group. If our essential task is to learn together what the world is really like, to see it in a Christian perspective and to have opportunities to engage in its political activities — then there is always a place to begin encouraging this process. It may be a conversation, a new experience in the life of the young person, a visit, a chance encounter. The beginnings may be humble and the process should never be forced. But for the discerning Christian youth worker the raw material of his trade is all around him in the youth group.

A Christian youth worker will not make his life easier by adopting even a tenth of the suggestions in this chapter. Tension and conflicts are the inevitable accompaniment of programmes of political education. But they may be a sign of vitality and the quest for maturity. In the Bible, when God speaks to men, they begin to argue with each other and with him! And we are not always grateful to our "emancipators" who want to open our eyes on the world as it is, thus shattering some of our comfortable illusions and giving us the onerous responsibility of freedom. When Pharaoh mustered his forces and pursued the children of Israel into the desert, many of the chosen began to pine for the security of bondage. "In their terror they clamoured to the Lord for help and said to Moses, 'Were there no graves in Egypt, that you should have brought us here to die in the wilderness? See what you have done to us by bringing us out of Egypt! Is not this what we meant when we said in Egypt: Leave us alone: let us be slaves to the Egyptians. We would rather be slaves to the Egyptians than die here in the wilderness.' "[17] Modern youth workers (through all their difficulties) can share with Moses the quiet conviction that they are offering those they serve the opportunity to become free men and women. More than that, if we are right about the Bible picture of God, they can be supported by the knowledge that they represent the mission and message of Christ on the modern scene, that they are trying to live in the Kingdom he announced. In the evolution of Christian experience, there can often be discerned three stages which may be described by three questions. "What did Christ do?" "What would Christ do?" "What is Christ doing?" The Christian youth worker who aspires to be a political educator tries to operate at the third stage.

Chapter notes

CHAPTER 1.

1. Max Weber: *The Protestant Ethic and the Spirit of Capitalism* (Scribner 1958)
2. John Kenneth Galbraith: *The Age of Uncertainty* (Andre Deutsch)
3. J. A. T. Robinson: *On being the Church in the World* (S.C.M.)
4. Mary Bosanquet: *The Life and Death of Dietrich Bonhoeffer* (Hodder & Stoughton)
5. Quoted from Alicia Perceval: *Youth will be Led* (Collins)
6. R. K. Merton: *Social Theory & Social Structure* (Free Press)
7. Hans Kung: *On being a Christian* (Collins)
8. M. Stacey: *Transition and Change: a study of Banbury* (Oxford U.P.)
9. This was an issue fully explored at the National Evangelical Conference on Social Ethics held at High Leigh Conference Centre, Hoddeston, September 1978. This conference represented a significant breakthrough; papers read at it are to be published by the Paternoster Press during 1980. For further details write to John Gladwin, Shaftesbury Project, 8 Oxford Street, Nottingham.
10. For useful material on this subject cf. David Sheppard: *Built as a City* (Hodder and Stoughton)

CHAPTER 2.

1. Bernard Crick: *In Defence of Politics* (Pelican)
2. Robert Stradling: *A Programme for Political Education. The Political Awareness of the School Leaver* (Hansard Society) p.54
3. Bernard Crick and Derek Heater: (Falmer Press): In particular, cf. three chapters in *Essays on Political Education*. 2.1 Basic political concepts and curriculum development; 2.2 Basic concepts for political education; 2.3 Procedural values in political education.
4. cf. Crick & Heater, *ibid*, I.4 "On bias".
5. Laurie Lee: *Cider with Rosie* (Penguin)
6. *The Youth Service in England & Wales* (H.M.S.O.)
7. *Document I. A programme for Political Education* (Hansard Society)

CHAPTER 3.

1. *The Future of Voluntary Organizations* (Report of the Wolfenden Committee) (Croon Helm)
2. S. Alinsky: *Reveille for Radicals* (Chicago University Press) and *Rules for Radicals* (Random House)
3. Amos 8:6
4. The word "myth" is used here, not with its common meaning as applied to something false; but signifying an allegory, a pictorial expression, cast in historical form, of a truth that it would be difficult to portray in prosaic form. Hence the significance of a religious myth does not depend on its historical accuracy nor is its meaning exhausted by the circumstances to which it gave rise. Most Christians today would not believe that there were actually two people called Adam and Eve who were our first parents. But they would claim that their story gives us, among other things, faithful insight into the true meaning and scope of human wrongdoing.
5. Donald A Hay: *A Christian Critique of Capitalism* (Grove Books)
6. Lesslie Newbigin: *Honest Religion for Secular Man* (S.C.M.)
7. W. F. Whyte: *Street Corner Society* (University of Chicago Press)

CHAPTER 4.

1. Emilio Castro: *Amidst Revolution* (Christian Journals, Belfast)
2. Radomiro Tomic: *Worldwide* volume 16 No. 7. 'No room for illusion'.
3. cf. James H. Cone: *God of the Oppressed: (S.P.C.K.)*
4. *cf. Rex Brico: Taize: Brother Roger and his Community* (Collins). A recent account. For the whole 'Christian commune' movement c.f. D. B. Clark: *Basic Communities* (S.P.C.K.)
5. Walter James: *The Rôle and Function of Voluntary Youth Organizations* (Methodist Church. Division of Education & Youth)
6. *ibid* p.13
7. A comprehensive list of the names and addresses of these organizations is given at the end of chapter 5.
8. cf. *Scouting and the Open Society* by David Loades and *Venture Scouting* Chapter 4.
9. cf. Bernard Davies and Alan Gibson: *The Social Education of the Adolescent* (University of London Press). Chapter 2, "A historical perspective".
10. Alicia Percival: *Youth will be led* (Collins)
11. cf. *Report on the encouragement of youth participation.* Report

of the working party of the Youth Service Forum (D.E.S.) 1978.
12. In a letter to the author.
13. United Reform Church. Youth Committees, 86 Tavistock Place, London, WC1 9RT. Youth Leaflet No. 7. cf. also their half-yearly publication *Goad and Youth Work: A statement of policy and principles.*
14. *Seven guiding principles for MAYC.*
15. cf. *Share International,* for example, produced three times a year. *Bridge-Building Resource Material* (The Methodist Association of Education & Youth, Chester House, Pages Lane, Muswell Hill, London N1 1PR)
16. *A Time for Building* issued (27/7/78) by the Catholic Youth Service Council.
       In addition to the denominations and organizations mentioned in this chapter, there are of course others who seek in their own way to provide programmes which will help their members to learn more about the world in which they are growing up. For a fuller list see the index.
17. Frontier Youth Trust, 47 Marylebone Lane, London W1M 6AX. These quotations are from copies of *Review* Nos. 6 & 7. cf. also their publication *Information Service,* issued quarterly. Another movement which, under pressure from immediate events, has developed a political consciousness is Corrymeela in Northern Ireland. cf. Alf McCreary: *Corrymeela — The Search for Peace* Christian Journals, Belfast).
18. Scripture Union, 47 Marylebone Lane, London W1M 6AX. cf. in particular their teaching material, *Teaching over 13s.*
19. cf. the publication *Towards Renewal* published by the Post Green Community, 57 Dorchester Road, Lytchett Minster, Dorset.
20. Alan Kreider, Director, 14 Shepherd's Hill, Highgate, London N.6.
21. *Political Education Broadsheet,* St. Andrew's Youth Centre, Halifax.
22. In a letter to the author from Ken Fleming, Leader of St. Andrew's Youth Centre, Halifax.
23. Paulo Freire: *Paedagogy of the Oppressed* (Herder & Herder)
24. Ian Fraser: *The Fire Runs* (SCM)
25. 'An alternative agenda for party politics'. *Guardian,* 3rd. July 1978.

CHAPTER 5.

1. cf. Tom Brennan and Jonathan E. Brown (ed.): *Teaching Politics: Problems & Perspectives* (B.B.C. Publications) pp 58ff,

"Contexts for Political Education".
2. 1 Samuel 3: 1-10
3. cf. *Frontier Youth Trust Review* No. 8.
4. cf. *inter alia* Bernard Crick and Derek Heater: *Essays on Political Education* (Falmer Press)
5. cf. Bill Cockell: *The Training of Voluntary Youth Workers* (Methodist Church, Division of Education & Youth) pp 67/8.
6. *Games and Simulations* (B.B.C. Publications)
7. T. R. Batten: *The Non-directive approach in Group & Community work* (Oxford) and *The Human factor in Youth Work* (Oxford)
8. John A. T. Robinson: *On being the Church in the World* (S.C.M.) p. 113.
9. Robinson, *ibid,* p. 114.
10. The *Guardian* has published a list of several hundred "pressure groups".
11. Sources of supply are listed at the end of this book.
12. British Youth Council, 57 Chalton Street, London NW1 1HU.
13. National Council for Voluntary Youth Services, 26 Bedford Square, London WC1B 3HU.
14. *Youth & Community Work in the 1970s.* (H.M.S.O.). (The Fairbairn-Milson Report).
15. *ibid,* paragraphs 160 and 165.
16. For further details write to Ken Fleming, St. Andrew's Youth Centre, Halifax. For more examples of youth participation in political affairs write to Secretary, Association of Community Workers, Chester Community Council, Watergate Street, Chester.
17. Exodus 14: 10-12 (N.E.B.)

Suggestions for further enquiry

Perhaps the most interesting feature of the literature mentioned below is that it comes from many different schools of thought within the Christian church, including, for example, Catholic and conservative evangelical sources. They share a conviction that Jesus came to announce a New Order affecting the whole of man's life and that believers are called to fight in God's name against all systems which mock his purposes for mankind. But it would be quite wrong to give the impression that the unanimity among politically-conscious Christians reaches to detailed agreement on policies and programmes. As usually happens, the movement of God's Spirit in our time has brought us a fresh set of complex perplexities. For instance, is democracy in any form always the system that Christians should support? How much attention ought Christians to devote to re-establishing the credibility of existing politicians? When should they seek alternative forms of government?

There are no immediate blue-print answers to these quandaries and any answer will only appear as Christians think and act together. These perplexities have not been fully explored in the present work, which is intended to be a primer on political education for Christians. Our invitation to young Christians is not to accept an agreed syllabus of Christian involvement but to discover in action together what such involvement should be, and the following books are intended as a "way in" for those concerned to provide the context for this learning.

'Older' books dealing with the socio-political implications of the Gospel
Harvey Cox: *The Secular City* (SCM)
Lesslie Newbigin: *Honest Religion for Secular Man* (SCM)
Reinhold Niebuhr: *Beyond Tragedy* (Nisbet)
Alan Richardson: *The Political Christ* (SCM)
J. A. T. Robinson: *On being the Church in the World* (SCM)
E. F. Schumacher: *Small is Beautiful* (Abacus)

More recent books on 'political theology'
James H. Cone: *God of the Oppressed* (SPCK)
Ian Fraser: *The Fire Burns* (SCM)
Paulo Freire: *Paedagogy of the Oppressed* (Penguin)
Gustav Gutierrez: *A Theology of Liberation* (SCM)
Helmut Gollwitzer: *The Christian Faith and the Marxist Criticism of Religion* (St. Andrew Press)
E. S. P. Jones: *Christian Engagement with Politics* (St. Andrew Press)
Alistair Kee (ed.): *A reader in Political Theology* (SCM)
Hans Kung: *On being a Christian* (Collins)
Stephen Major: *Paradise Defined: the Nature of Christian Society* (SPCK)
Jurgen Moltmann: *Religion, Revolution and the Future* (Scribner)
E. R. Norman: *Christianity and the World Order* (Oxford University Press)
Camilo Tores: *Revolutionary Priest* (Penguin)

General works on political education
F. W. G. Benemy: *Teaching British Government* (Dent)
Tom Brennan: *Political Studies. A handbook for teachers* (Longman)
Tom Brennan & Jonathan E. Brown (ed.): *Teaching Politics: Problems and Perspectives* (B.B.C. Publications)
Bernard Crick & Derek Heater: *Essays on Political Education* (Falmer)
H. Entwistle: *Political Education in a Democracy* (Routledge)
D. B. Heater: *The Teaching of Politics* (Methuen)
Robert Stradling: *The Political Awareness of the School Leavers* (Hansard Society)

Two related movements are devoted to the political education of the young. Their useful papers and pamphlets are available on application.
The Hansard Society, 12 Gower Street, London WC1P 6OP.
The Politics Association, 7 Hornbrook Grove, Solihull, West Midlands. (Monthly publication: *Teaching Politics).*

The 'community development' movement
Community Work and Social Change (Longman)
Current Issues in Community Work (Routledge & Kegan Paul)
Community Work One (Routledge & Kegan Paul)
Community Work Two (Routledge & Kegan Paul)
Fred Milson: *An Introduction to Community Work* (Routledge & Kegan Paul)

Resources

General

British Youth Council, 57 Chalton Street, London NW1 1HU.
Hansard Society, 12 Gower Street, London WC1E 6DP.
Labour Party, Young Socialists, Transport House, Smith Square, London SW1P 3JA.
National Council for Voluntary Youth Services, 26 Bedford Square, London WC1B 3HU.
National League of Young Liberals, National Liberal Club, 1 Whitehall Place, London SW1A 2HA.
National Youth Bureau, 37 Belvoir Street, Leicester LE1 6SL.
Politics Association, Sec., G. Beaven, 7 Queensway, Alsager, Stoke-on-Trent, Staffs.
Socialist Education Association, 184 Tressilian Road, Brockley, London SE4.
World Development Movement, Bedford Chambers, Covent Garden, London WC2E 8HA.
Young Communist League, 16 King Street, London WC2E 8HY.
Young Conservative Organization, 32 Smith Square, London SW1P 3HH.
Young Fabians, c/o The Fabian Society, 11 Dartmouth Street, London SW1H 9BN.

Inter-denominational, ecumenical Christian organizations concerned with political education and/or action

British Council of Churches, Youth Department, 10 Eaton Gate, London SW1W 9BT.
Christians Against Racism and Fascism, 1 Finch Road, Birmingham 19.
Christian Aid, P.O. Box 1, London SW1.
Christian Education Movement, Chester House, Pages Lane, London N10.
Christian Socialist Movement, Kingsway Hall, London WC2.
Evangelical Alliance, 19 Draycott Place, London SW3 2SJ.
Festival of Light, 21A Down Street, London W1Y 7DN.
Frontier Youth Trust, 47 Marylebone Lane, London W1M 6AX.

Inter-School Christian Fellowship, 47 Marylebone Lane, London W1M 6AX.
Order of Christian Unity, 35 Victoria Street, London SW1.
Post Green Community, 57 Dorchester Road, Lytchett Minster, Poole, Dorset, BH16 6JE.
Scripture Union, 47 Marylebone Lane, London W1M 6AX.
Shaftesbury Project: Details from John Gladwin, 8 Oxford Street, Nottingham.
Tear Fund, 1 Bridgeman Road, Teddington, Middlesex TW11 9AT.

Denominational

Catholic Youth Service Council, 41 Cromwell Road, London SW7.
Church of England Board of Education, Church House, Dean's Yard, Westminster, London SE1P 3NZ.
Department of Education & Youth, The Methodist Church, Chester House, Pages Lane, Muswell Hill, London N10 1PZ.
Division of Social Responsibility of the Methodist Church, 1 Central Buildings, Matthew Parker Street, London SW1H 9NH.
United Reformed Church, 86 Tavistock Place, London WC1.
Young People's Department, Baptist Union, Baptist Church House, 4 Southampton Row, London WC1B 4AB.

Increasingly, the missionary societies of the various denominations are being involved in "politics". Their addresses can be obtained from The British Council of Churches, 10 Eaton Gate, London SW1W 9BT.

For the address of any voluntary youth movements, write to Mr. Paul Miller, National Council for Voluntary Youth Services, 26 Bedford Square, London WC1B 3HU.

Periodicals

Corrymeela News, published bi-monthly. Corrymeela House, 8 Upper Crescent, Belfast, BT7 1NT.
Goad, issued through "FURY" (Fellowship of United Reformed Youth), 86 Tavistock Place, London WC1 9Rt.
Periscope, youth magazine of the British Council of Churches, 10 Eaton Gate, London SW1W 9BT.

Review and *News,* issued by Frontier Youth Trust, 47 Marylebone Lane, London W1M 6AX.

Risk, magazine of the youth department of the World Council of Churches. Obtainable from the British Council of Churches (see above).

Third Way, published fortnightly by the Thirty Press in association with the Evangelical Alliance: 19 Draycott Place, London SW3 2SJ.

Time for God, a voluntary scheme shared by several churches. Details from Free Church Federal Council: 27 Tavistock Square, London WC1H 9HH.

Towards Renewal, published quarterly by the Post Green Community and the Communities of Celebration: 57 Dorchester Road, Lytchett Minster, Poole, Dorset BH16 6JE.

Viewpoint, a magazine for sixth formers published by the Inter-School Christian Fellowship: 22 Lower Hillgate, Stockport, Cheshire SK1 1JE. (In particular — *Viewpoint 39.)*

Films

Granada Television Film Library, Manchester M60 9EA:

Has for hire three programmes of the 1973 series "State of the Nation".

Write also for details of their 6-part series *Politics — what's it all about?,* broadcast 1978 and 1979.

Concord Films, Nacton, Ipswich, Suffolk 1P10 0JZ, are specialists in films about contemporary problems.

The following sources also include in their catalogues films relevant to political education:

Film Forum Ltd., 56 Brewer Street, London W1R 3PA.

Guild Sound and Vision, Woodston House, Dundle Road, Peterborough PE2 9PZ.

Scottish Central Film Library, 16-17 Woodside Terrace, Charing Cross, Glasgow G37XN.

Short Bibliography: "How to do it".

J. P. Leighton: *Self-government in the Youth Group* NAYC

Various papers from Ken Fleming, St. Andrew's Youth Centre, Huddersfield Road, Halifax.

Teaching booklets from Scripture Union, 47 Marylebone Lane, London W1M 6AX.

Programmes of Political Education for Church Youth Groups — a leaflet from the Methodist Association of Youth Clubs, 2 Chester House, Pages Lane, London N10 1PR.

Causes which require some political action for their success
These are the addresses of the national headquarters. Many of these organizations have regional and local branches as well.

Citizens rights
Consumer Association, 14 Buckingham Street, London WC2N 6DS.
Minority Rights Group, 36 Craven Street, London WC2.
National Council for Civil Liberties, 186 King's Cross Road, London N1 9NJ.

Community Service
Community Service Volunteers, 273 Pentonville Road, London N1 9NJ.
Task Force, Clifford House, Edith Villas, London W14 8UG.
Young Volunteer Force Foundation, 7 Leonard Street, London EC2.

Conservation
Conservation Society, 21 Hanyards Lane, Cuffley, Potters Bar, Herts.
Friends of the Earth, 8 King Street, London WC2.
Noise Abatement Society, 6-8 Old Bond Street, London W1.

Deprivation
CHAR (Campaign for the Homeless and the Rootless), 27 Endell Street, London WC2.

Family Life
Family Service Units, 207 Old Marylebone Road, London NW1 TQP.
Family Welfare Association, 501-5 Kingsland Road, London E8 4AU.
Gingerbread (for one-parent families), 9 Poland Street, London W1V 3DG.
National Council for One-Parent Families, 255 Kentish Town Road, London NW5.

Fight against disease
Cancer Research Campaign, 2 Carlton House, Terrace, London SW1Y 5AR.
Mind (National Association for Mental Health), 22 Harley Street, London W1N 2ED.

Help for the aged
Age Concern, Bernard Sunley House, 60 Pitcairn Road, Mitcham, Surrey CR4 3LL.
Help the Aged, 8 Denman Street, London W1A 2AP.

Help for the handicapped and disabled
British Council for Rehabilitation of the Disabled, Tavistick House South, Tavistick Square, London WC1H 9LB.
Federation of Gateway Clubs, Pembridge Hall, Pembridge Square, London W2 4EP.

PHAB (Physically Handicapped & Able-Bodied),
30 Devonshire Street, London W1N 2AP.
Royal National Institution for the Blind, 224-6 Gt. Portland Street,
London W1N 6AA.
Royal National Institution for the Deaf, 105 Gower Street,
London WC1E 6AH.

Homelessness
Shelter, 86 The Strand, London WC2R 0EQ.

International
Amnesty International, 55 Theobald's Road, London WC1X 8SP.
Oxfam, 274 Banbury Road, Oxford OX2 7DZ.
Save the Children Fund, 157 Clapham Road, London SW9 0PT.
War on Want, 467 Caledonian Road, London N7 9BE.
Voluntary Service Overseas, 14 Bishop's Bridge Road,
London W26AA.

Offenders
Howard League for Penal Reform, 125 Kensington Park Road,
London SE11.
NACRO (National Association for the Care & Resettlement of
Offenders), 125 Kensington Park Road, London SE11.
PROP (Preservation of Rights of Prisoners), 339a Finchley Road,
London NW3.
RAP (Radical Alternatives to Prison), Eastbourne House,
Bullards Place, London E2.

Racial Equality
Anti-Apartheid Movement, 89 Charlotte Street, London W1P 2DQ.
Commission for Racial Equality, Elliott House,
10-12 Allington Street, London SW1E.
Institution of Race Relations, 36 Jermyn Street, London W1.
Joint Council for the Welfare of Immigrants, 55 Theobald's Road,
London, WC1X 8SP.

The degree to which these organizations are pressure groups varies.
They are only a small selection. A fuller list can be found in Sheila
Moore's *Working for Free* (Pan).

Index of Authors

Index of Subjects